Writers in Windsor

Hester Davenport was born in Plymouth, but has lived in Old Windsor since 1964. She has worked as a teacher of English, mainly in adult education. Recently she has become interested in writing and has published a number of articles and in 1993 a children's book, *The Early Times Book of Unsolved Mysteries* (Puffin Books). She has a number of hobbies, including pottery, screen-printing, theatre, music, and fair-weather gardening. She is married, with two daughters.

Church Street leading to Windsor Castle

Hester Davenport

Hester Davenport

Writers in Windsor

Illustrated by

Michael H.H. Bayley ARIBA
and
Olivia Davenport

Cell Mead Press

Published 1995
Reprinted 1996

Cell Mead Press
60 Church Road
Old Windsor
Berkshire

ISBN 0 9526678 0 0

Set in Times New Roman 11 point

Printed in Great Britain by
Thameslink Ltd, Windsor

To

Tony,
Imogen and Olivia

Key to the cover illustration:

1. Edward Lear (and p.103) 2. Mary Shelley (p.83) 3. Edith Wharton (p.117) 4. P.B. Shelley 5. Henry Howard, Earl of Surrey 6. H.G. Wells (p.127) 7. Thomas Hardy 8. Samuel Pepys 9. Charles Knight (p.143) 10. Edith Wharton's 'Chariot of Fire' (p.121) 11. Samuel Johnson 12. Geoffrey Chaucer (below and p.139) 13. Charles Dickens (p.91) 14. Celia Fiennes (p.38) 15. Oscar Wilde (p.110) 16. Fanny Burney 17. Henry James 18. Jonathan Swift 19. George Orwell 20. William Shakespeare (p.147)

Original drawings by Michael Bayley:

Cover, frontispiece, left, and pages 12, 26, 38, 76, 83, 88, 91, 103, 110, 117, 121, 127, 139, 143, 147.

Original drawings by Olivia Davenport:

pages 14, 20, 21, 30, 32, 34, 46, 49, 51, 55, 57, 59, 61, 71, 73, 77, 81, 85, 92, 94, 96, 99, 104, 109, 113, 115, 124, 131, 134, 136.

Illustrations on pages 27, 45, 79 and 114 are by W. Alfred Delamotte from Harrison Ainsworth's *Windsor Castle*, 1843; on pages 81,129 and 132 from Richard S. Chattock's *Sketches of Eton*, 1874, on page 25 from Charles Knight's *Pictorial Shakespeare*, 1843, and on page 42 from *Magna Britannia* by Daniel Lysons, 1813.

CONTENTS

**[...]—denotes writer of minor importance in the chapter*

Acknowledgements

The silhouette of George III and his family on page 63 is reproduced by gracious permission of Her Majesty the Queen. The picture of the Princess Royal at All Saints' Church on page 108 is reproduced by permission of the *Illustrated London News* Picture Library; that of the River Thames on page 65 by permission of Clewer Museum. The author acknowledges the generosity of the above in waiving reproduction fees.

The silhouette of Dorothy Wordsworth on page 68 is published by permission of The Wordsworth Trust.

Quotations from Queen Victoria's *Journal* are with the gracious permission of Her Majesty the Queen. The quotation from Edward Lear's letter is by kind permission of the Huntington Library, San Marino, California. The Oxford University Press has given permission to quote from a number of its publications: *The Early Letters of William and Dorothy Wordsworth*, edited by Ernest de Selincourt (1935), *The Collected Letters of Charles Dickens*, edited by Madeline House and Graham Storey (1988), *The Letters of Percy Bysshe Shelley*, edited by Frederick L. Jones (1964), and *Jonathan Swift: Journal to Stella*, edited by Harold Williams (1974).

The author also acknowledges a debt to all publishers and authors from whose works, cited in the *Bibliography*, quotations and information are drawn, without which this book could not have been written.

Introduction

This book is full of anecdotes of the great and famous, but I shall begin with one of my own.

I first visited the Windsor area in November of 1955, when a student of Literature at University College London. The English Department held a weekend conference at Cumberland Lodge in the Great Park, and the beautiful old red-brick building and magnificent parkland around were very refreshing after London's grit and grime. With others I went on Sunday morning to the service in the Royal Chapel attached to Royal Lodge. Afterwards, in the sunshine, we watched five-year-old Princess Anne skipping unselfconsciously amongst the fallen autumn leaves, wearing a bright blue coat and bonnet, with golden curls under the brim haloing her face.

Later that day I fancied a walk by myself in the Park, and though evening was drawing in and the mists were rising I set off, following a path which ran along the fence of Royal Lodge and then climbed upwards. Suddenly I had a shock: rising out of the gloomy mists in front was a great figure on horse-back. We'd joked the previous evening about the headless ghost of Herne the Hunter, to look on whom was death; this rider had his head firmly on his shoulders, but I certainly felt an instant's panic before I realised what it was. I had had my first meeting with George III on his Copper Horse.

This mixture of person, event, buildings, landscapes, royalty and literature is what this book is about. I didn't at first realise, when I came to live and teach in the Windsor area in the mid 1960s, just how many literary connections it had. Of course I had come across some of the writings which draw on Windsor and its history. There was, for example, Harrison Ainsworth's historical romance of 1843, *Windsor Castle*, which with a good deal of artistic licence recreates the reign of Henry VIII and uses the Herne the Hunter legend, as also does Shakespeare's *The Merry Wives of Windsor*. Then there were poems which speak admiringly of the landscape of Castle, Park and Thames, such as Pope's 'Windsor Forest'; in that poem Pope makes it clear that he sees himself as part of a tradition of poets who took the Windsor landscape for inspiration.

Of a completely different character is Jerome K.Jerome's *Three Men in a Boat* of 1889. This comic classic of Thames exploration stages literature's greatest vanishing act, when after he has talked of Runnymede, King John and

Magna Carta, and praised the ale at the Bells of Ouseley pub at Old Windsor, Jerome disposes of town and Castle with a mere flick of his pen:

> After you pass Old Windsor, the river is somewhat uninteresting, and does not become itself again until you are nearing Boveney.

H.G. Wells also performed a conjuring trick with Windsor Castle, when in his 1923 novel *Men Like Gods* characters who are driving along with it in their sights are suddenly transported to another road in another world.

These were writings I'd come across; I also laughed a lot at Beryl Bainbridge's black comedy *The Bottle Factory Outing*, when it was published in 1974. It tells of a picnic in the Great Park which goes horribly wrong, leaving the picnickers with a body they don't know what to do with: as a short term expedient they take their cars, with the body propped up in the back of one of them, for a drive round the Safari Park—a tourist attraction to rival the Castle then.

This didn't make up a large body of "Windsor" literature, but I slowly came to realise what a number of our most famous writers had interesting personal connections with the town. Often I would find myself in classes saying "This writer has a Windsor connection..." There were Chaucer and Shakespeare to begin with; then, among others, the poet Shelley who made return visits with a different woman in tow. Thomas Hardy came to build a church and half fell in love with a princess, H.G. Wells was a rebellious apprentice in the drapery business, and Henry James got wordily lost in King's Road.

I discovered that the Victorian novelist Margaret Oliphant, whose *Miss Marjoribanks* I admired for its social comedy, had lived for thirty years in Clarence Crescent in the heart of the town, though at the time very few in Windsor seemed to have heard of her.

So it was that I got drawn into discovering more famous authors who had come to Windsor or its Castle, to visit or to live. It was intriguing to find that a number of them had made memorable records of what they did and saw in letters, journals or autobiographies, and to discover how these Windsor experiences fitted in with their lives and work as a whole.

These miniature biographies, glimpses into their lives and into Windsor's and England's past, are the result. I haven't tried to include every author who ever set foot in Windsor, and have excluded lesser-known writers unless they connect with major ones. But I am sorry not to have found a place for Perdita

Robinson, poet, actress, and mistress of the Prince Regent, whose beauty is preserved in paintings by Gainsborough, Reynolds and Romney, and whose grave is in Old Windsor churchyard not far from where I sit. This note must make brief amends. I have crossed the Thames a few times into Eton and included writers who were at school there and for whom Windsor was in adult life of some significance, but a full literary history of Eton College would require a book of its own.

I could not have produced this book without a great deal of help from others, to all of whom I am indebted.

Firstly I must thank my family. The idea for the book came originally from my husband Tony, and he has been extremely supportive during its writing, making suggestions and discovering new writers for me. He has also shown great tolerance in the invasion of his study.

My daughter Olivia has spent many hours working on drawings for the book, both of buildings and people. I feel proud of her work, as well as very grateful to her for her efforts.

My elder daughter Imogen, and Matthew Low, have been very helpful and patient in setting up computer programmes and answering my squeals for help. Without them the computing would have been an uphill struggle.

I first saw some of Michael Bayley's fine drawings at a meeting of the Friends of the Royal Borough Collection. When I introduced myself to him and pressed on him the idea of designing a cover for a book he'd never heard of, he listened with great courtesy and good nature and agreed to help. The result speaks for itself, and I am immensely grateful to him for the work, and for allowing me to use other of his drawings.

Without the enthusiasm and interest of Alison Haymonds in the book, it would certainly have been still-born. She has given me great encouragement in the writing, and been most generous with professional advice about printing and publishing. I am greatly in her debt.

Friends in the Windsor Local History Publications Group have also been most supportive. I am grateful to all of them for their encouragement, but would like to mention particularly Sheila Rooney who kindly read the text and offered valuable publishing advice, and Gordon Cullingham, Ellen Dollery,

Beryl Hedges and Joyce Sampson for information and help. I am grateful also to Dr Judith Hunter for allowing me access to the Royal Borough Collection.

I must thank John Handcock of the Royal Albert Institute Trust for reading the book with interest and care; all errors are my responsibility, but the book is the better for his many helpful suggestions.

The interest shown in my talks to the Windsor and Eton Society encouraged me greatly in writing the book, and I should like to thank the Chairman, Dr John Long, and the Society for inviting me to speak to them.

To Professor W.M. Russell I am grateful for much fascinating material about Herne the Hunter. I wish I could have made greater use of it.

Thanks are owed to Mary Francis of The Priory, and Major and Mrs Murrough O'Brien of Shelley's House, for kindly allowing me to see and photograph their houses.

I am most grateful for help given me in converting a disk by Noel Heather of Royal Holloway College, and the Computer Department of the College for their assistance with graphics.

Finally I must offer warmest thanks to the sponsors of this book—the Royal Albert Institute Trust, and the Windsor Local History Publications Group—fairy godmothers who have helped transform a manuscript into a published book.

The Copper Horse

CHAPTER ONE

Royal Servant and Royal Prisoner

Geoffrey Chaucer (134?-1400), James I of Scotland (1394-1437)

FOR NINE HUNDRED YEARS Windsor Castle and Windsor town have grown up together. The Castle came first, established on a chalk cliff above the Thames by William the Conqueror as one of a number of military strongholds to enforce his seizure of the throne from the Anglo-Saxon kings. But over the centuries the red and grey-roofed houses of the town which clung below its western walls fanned out from the massive grey fortress above, creating an independent community. The Saxon King Edward the Confessor had also built a palace on low-lying ground near the Thames a mile or so further down stream; for a while the Norman kings continued to use this too, but soon the Castle became not only a fortress but a favourite royal residence, and the palace at what came to be known as Old Windsor was abandoned.

Kings were always on the move then, taking the whole apparatus of court and government with them from one palace to another. After a few weeks in each, the twin problems of food supply and waste disposal for a huge army of courtiers, administrators, clergy and servants, required that wagons be loaded up again to jolt along rough roads to the next port of call. Windsor Castle was one of the most-visited of the early kings' homes because of the hunting in Windsor Forest. The Castle became a chosen venue for special occasions such as Christmas, and the kings developed, extended and ornamented the Castle until by the reign of King Edward III it had become one of the finest buildings in Europe.

Edward III was born in the Castle in 1312 and christened in what was then St Edward's Chapel (built by his great-grandfather King Henry III in honour of Edward the Confessor). A powerful warrior king who also loved pageantry and ceremonial, he looked back in admiration to the imagined days of King Arthur and the chivalry of the Knights of the Round Table. In 1348 he formed the Order of the Garter for his own knights, and thus established a tradition which continues to this day (the reason for his curious choice of a garter as symbol is obscure: the story of the King gallantly redeeming the embarrassment of the Countess of Salisbury when she lost hers while dancing is probably apocryphal). St George was named as patron saint of the new order, and St Edward's Chapel refurbished and given an additional dedication which amounted to re-naming. A tradition of splendid festivities on and around St George's Day (23 April) was established, with processions, services, jousting tournaments, lavish feasting, dancing and music. Though the ceremony no longer takes place on St George's Day, the tourists and citizens of Windsor who throng to see the Queen and her Garter Knights, wearing their dark blue robes and processing down through the Lower Ward to St George's Chapel, are witnessing a ritual which has survived seven hundred years of turbulent history.

It seems appropriate that the first recorded occasion when a literary figure is connected with Windsor is on a St George's Day. The year was 1357, just nine years after the Garter Order was founded, and the writer Geoffrey Chaucer. He is known as the father of English Literature for his use of English for works like *The Canterbury Tales,* written at a time when French was still the language of the court and regarded as culturally superior. But in 1357 Geoffrey was only a boy, a page in the household of the Countess of Ulster.

No-one knows the exact date of his birth, but it seems likely that he was between fourteen and sixteen years old in 1357. John Chaucer, his father, was a prosperous London merchant who at the time of his son's birth was Deputy Butler to King Edward III. This didn't mean that he was a kind of medieval Jeeves, but that he was responsible for importing and stocking the wine for the King's cellar. He had no aristocratic blood but he moved in the royal circle and was clearly anxious that his son should do the same. It was then the fashion for noblemen's sons to join some other grand household to receive the

Geoffrey Chaucer

proper education for future court life, and John Chaucer did well in gaining for his son a position with the wife of Edward III's second son.

Like the Queen, the Countess had an entourage distinct from her husband's, with at least one clerk, chaplain, squire, yeoman of the chamber, and at the bottom of the pecking order one or more pages. In return for attending to his duties, young Geoffrey would have been given food, clothes, lodging and also training, probably including academic tuition from the chaplain or clerk, but mainly concentrating on military and social skills. He'd have learnt how to ride and to handle weapons and, just as importantly, the manners and behaviour required of a courtier.

It is only by chance that we know of the boy at this time. A book containing poetry by two later writers was found to have in its binding leaves from the Countess's household account book, covering the period from July 1356 to January 1359. The name "Galfrido Chaucer" is found in an entry for April 1357 which records that the Countess paid four shillings (20p) for a paltock for him (a paltock was a short jacket such as pages wore), and three shillings for a pair of shoes and some red and black hose. These new clothes would have been bought for the celebration of Easter in London on 9 April, but perhaps we can picture him wearing the same smart parti-coloured tights for the St George's Day festivities two weeks later.

He'd have been kept busy in attendance at the sumptuous banquets which the King served up to his knights as reward for their loyalty, and as a sign of both his munificence and magnificence. Pages had to be aware of the appropriate rituals involved in serving at table, and conscious too of niceties of rank. They had to learn the correct forms of address, and the proper kind of talk, especially to ladies. At a more basic level they were expected to keep hands and finger-nails clean, and neither to pick their noses, spit or scratch themselves, nor to touch the dogs that would be waiting under the tables for scraps to fall.

It's a pity that in his writings the older Chaucer doesn't describe ceremonies which we might identify with those of the court of Edward III. Perhaps they were just too familiar to him and his courtly audience. In *The Knight's Tale* he does briefly give some sense of a great feast, though it is while telling his audience that he's *not* going to describe the scene. In this chivalrous romance the noble Duke Theseus, who must come near to representing the image cultivated by King Edward III and his son the Black Prince, entertains an assembly of knights on the eve of a great tournament (jousting was part of the

A medieval feast

St George's Day celebrations too). Chaucer says that Theseus feasted and entertained his guests lavishly, and worked so hard to honour them that it would have been impossible to do more. He goes on (the spellings have been modernised):

> The minstralcy, the service at the feast,
> The great gifts to the most and least,
> The rich array of Theseus' palace,
> Nor who sat first or last upon the dais,
> What ladies fairest been or best dancing,
> Or which of them can dancen best or sing,
> Nor who most feelingly speaketh of love;
> What hawks sit on the perch above,
> What hounds lie on the floor adown,
> Of all this make I now no mention.

It is a sketchy picture, but still manages to suggest a little of what the atmosphere of the St George's Day feast of 1357 might have been.

As he grew older Chaucer must have taken part in many more such occasions, since he climbed steadily up the royal service ladder, till he reached the top by becoming King Edward's "beloved valettus". Again the modern connotations of a valet don't give a true idea of his responsibilities, which seem to have been those of a trusted emissary. In 1368 a licence to travel to the continent from Dover was issued to Chaucer, "donne souz nostre prive seal a Wyndesore" (official documents were written in French or Latin). We don't know what he did there, but we do know that in the years which followed he frequently travelled on the King's business in Europe, sometimes on commercial matters, sometimes engaged in secret missions.

At the same time he was winning a reputation for himself as a writer. Printing had not yet been invented, so his audience would have listened to rather than read his works: there are pictures of Chaucer in the margins of manuscripts (dating from after his death but seeming to capture an individual face), rotund in middle age, a pointing finger thrusting forward as if in active delivery of his tales. It would be nice to imagine that a reading of one of them, *The Knight's Tale* perhaps with its story of two knights contesting for a beautiful lady, took place sometime in St George's Hall as part of the Garter festivities. Then the pointing finger might, as he spoke, have picked out the fairest lady, the best dancer, she who spoke most feelingly of love.

We get some impression of the personality of Geoffrey Chaucer from his writings: he was clearly a man with a good sense of humour, and an engaging line in self-deprecation, but none of the true materials of biography such as letters, memoirs or anecdotes exist. References in official documents give us facts but nothing else. One wonders what Chaucer's feelings were about some of the posts he held, such as that of Clerk of the King's Works.

A warrant authorising Chaucer's appointment to this post was issued "a nostre chastel de Wyndesore" on 12 July 1389 by King Richard II, who had succeeded his grandfather Edward III in 1377. For a payment of two shillings a day (10p), Chaucer was made responsible for the management of building and maintenance works for all the King's properties, with the exception of Windsor Castle. However, a year later another warrant placed St George's Chapel in Chaucer's care too. The reason for the transference becomes clear when the document states that the Chapel "est en poynt du ruyne et de cheier a la terre": it was on the point of collapse. Putting the building in the Clerk's control meant that bills for the necessary repairs would fall on the exchequer, not the Castle.

Chaucer was ordered to employ carpenters and other workmen, set them to work, and procure all necessary materials for the repairs. (Workmen, like sailors in a later age, were impressed into the King's service with no right of refusal, and as Clerk Chaucer was required to apprehend any who absconded, or stole the materials.) He is recorded spending £100.17s.4d., a large sum then, on 101 tons of Stapleton stone and 200 cartloads of Reigate stone for the Chapel. But after the carts had trundled up the hill and dumped the stone it seems that little was done with it, for a few years later it was used by Chaucer's successor as Clerk not for the Chapel, but in repairing other royal properties.

A year after Chaucer assumed responsibility for St George's Chapel, the Clerkship was taken from him. We don't know why, or whether he heaved a sigh of relief at being rid of the job. Quite probably he did, for he was growing older and the post involved a great deal of travelling around the country. Since he had to carry money to pay wages he was at risk from thieves too, and was indeed attacked and robbed on several occasions. Whether he was good at the job or not, it brought him a fair amount of bother.

After he'd given it up Chaucer went into honourable retirement. He had time then to give to writing *The Canterbury Tales*, fortified no doubt by an annual grant of a tun of wine from Richard II. As for St George's Chapel, it fell into greater and greater disrepair until in 1478 Edward IV ordered its demolition. It was replaced by the magnificent building which stands today.

ꟾ

The success of Geoffrey Chaucer encouraged others to follow in his footsteps, and one of the next generation of writers was a King, connected both unhappily and happily with Windsor. King James I of Scotland suffered imprisonment in the Castle, but he also fell in love there and made a very happy marriage.

James was only eleven when in 1406 he was sent to the French court for his education by his father, the King of Scotland. Unluckily the ship was intercepted off the Yorkshire coast by pirates who realised what a prize they'd obtained. When he heard the news James's father collapsed and died, thereby increasing the boy's value as the new King of Scotland. When he was brought south to the court of Henry IV the English king might have demanded a high ransom (it was the custom to ransom captured men of rank, and Edward III had once contributed £16 to redeem Chaucer from the French), but instead he sent him to the Tower of London, reputedly remarking that James could learn French just as well in England as in France.

After a while James' position as a state prisoner became easier; he was brought to the court and spent time at various royal residences including Windsor. His education was not neglected and like Chaucer he learnt all the military, social and scholarly skills appropriate to nobility. It was at Windsor Castle on St George's Day 1421 that he received knighthood. But before this date the political situation had changed. When Henry IV was dying in 1413 he is said to have urged his heir to release the Scottish King, now an adult. Instead Henry V sent him back to the Tower under conditions of harsh and miserable poverty. Only when it suited Henry's purposes was James displayed in finery as a "most dear" relation.

Luckily for James, Henry V died in 1422 and the conditions of his imprisonment then eased. He was again at Windsor when he fell in love with an English noblewoman descended from Edward III, Lady Joan Beaufort. He describes the experience in his autobiographical poem, *The Kingis Quair* (The King's Book), written either then or when he returned to Scotland.

James must have known the works of Chaucer, as his book has a very Chaucerian flavour. He records his journey on the "wawis [waves] weltering to and fro", followed by the misery and despair of capture and imprisonment. Then one day, like the princes in Chaucer's *The Knight's Tale*, he looks out from the window of the tower onto a garden below (spellings modernised):

> Now was there made, fast by the tower's wall,
> A garden fair, and in the corners set
> An arbour green, with wands long and small
> Railed about, and so with trees beset
> Was all the place, and hawthorn hedges knet [*intertwined*]
> That life was none awalking there forby
> That might scarce any wight espy. [*person*]
>
> So thick the branches and the leaves green,
> Beshaded all the alleys that there were,
> And midst of every arbour might be seen
> The sharp, green, sweet juniper,
> Growing so fair, with branches here and there,
> That as it seemed to a life without
> The bows spread the arbour all about.

Into the beautiful garden comes an equally beautiful maiden, with whom the prisoner falls instantly in love.

Windsor historians would like James to have been specific about which tower he was in, but *The Kingis Quair* is not that kind of poem. The garden he describes may be imaginary, but it is likely that he is giving us a picture of an actual one, laid out formally in the fashion of the times, with an arbour in a corner, a wooden picket fence, and neat hawthorn hedges.

Coinciding with James' discovery of love came negotiations for his release. The English drove a hard bargain and demanded a huge ransom, but finally in 1424, a month after marriage to Lady Joan Beaufort and eighteen years after his enforced arrival on English soil, James I was able to ride north and claim his kingdom. He was to prove an able ruler, owing something at least to his many years of English education.

CHAPTER TWO

Proud Courtiers

Henry Howard, Earl of Surrey (1517-47),
William Shakespeare (1564-1616), Sir Walter Ralegh (1554-1618)

Henry Howard, Earl of Surrey

IN THE TURBULENT second half of the fifteenth century, noble was pitted against noble when rival claimants to the throne clashed in the bloody civil war known as the Wars of the Roses. The subsequent victory of Henry VII and the establishment of the Tudor dynasty brought back stability to the kingdom, and courtiers were able to turn their attention to thoughts of love instead of war. The ability to turn out a sonnet in praise of a mistress's beauty became as much of a gentlemanly accomplishment as skilled sword play. The court was a dangerous place though, as nobles vied between themselves for royal favour which, heady when possessed, could when lost lead swiftly to the executioner's block. The sudden turning of Fortune's wheel, precipitating men from eminence to disgrace, was to be a theme of Shakespeare's plays, and the saying "pride goes before a fall" is well illustrated by the careers of two courtier-poets, Henry Howard Earl of Surrey, and Sir Walter Ralegh.

Henry Howard was a nobleman for whose life during the reign of Henry VIII it would be possible to make a graph recording the peaks and troughs; like James I he was to know Windsor Castle as place of both pleasure and prison. Once described as the "most foolish proud boy that is in England", he was the dashing son of the wealthy Duke of Norfolk, tracing his ancestry back to the early kings of England, a pride that in the end cost him his life. In portraits Surrey is seen, splendidly dressed, arrogance radiating from his confident stance and haughty look. Shakespeare's lines of half a century later, in which Ophelia describes Prince Hamlet as courtier, soldier, scholar,

The glass of fashion and the mould of form,
The expectancy and rose of the fair state

could perfectly be applied to Surrey (in fact they fit him rather better than they do Hamlet). He was also an innovative poet, the first to make use in English of the 14-lined Italian sonnet form, and the creator of the blank verse which Shakespeare used for his plays.

As a boy Surrey was a favourite of Henry VIII, a monarch whose strength and power seems reflected in the architecture of the massive Henry VIII Gateway to Windsor Castle. His court was a brilliant one, but as in medieval times moving restlessly from palace to palace: at Windsor the hunting was prized as before, and there were facilities for all the favourite royal sports including tennis, jousting and archery. Magnificent banquets were served, the Garter ceremonies were great occasions, and there was music, dancing, and

Henry VIII Gateway

entertainment from the King's jesters. Henry Howard was to become one of the brightest satellites of the glittering court, with a reputation which spread throughout Europe, but when he was only thirteen Henry chose him to be companion at Windsor Castle to his eleven-year-old son born out of wedlock, Henry Fitzroy the Duke of Richmond. The two youths became close friends for the rest of Richmond's short life (he died of tuberculosis six years later), spending much of that time together at the Castle.

This was the period when Henry was trying to put aside his wife Catherine of Aragon for her failure to provide him with a legitimate son and heir; he'd also fallen in love with one of Catherine's waiting women, Surrey's cousin Anne Boleyn. Surrey was at the Castle on the July day in 1531 when Henry rode off on a hunting expedition with Anne from which he did not return; Catherine never saw the King again. Eighteen months later when the long-delayed marriage to Anne was celebrated, up went the Howard family's fortunes. But her fall from grace after failing to produce a son, and subsequent execution on charges of adultery, brought them into disfavour too.

Jane Seymour, another waiting gentlewoman who had caught the King's eye, became Queen, and her relatives moved into the positions of power, loathed and resented as upstarts by the Howards. In 1537, the year after the deaths of both Anne and Richmond, there occurred an incident at Hampton Court when Surrey struck out at Edward Seymour, Jane's brother. The attack had been provoked but it was risky, since according to the courtly code of conduct Surrey could have been punished by having his arm cut off.

Fortunately for him he was sent instead to cool his heels at Windsor Castle. Here the memories of the years with Richmond added to his wretchedness. In an untitled poem of lamentation written then, Surrey contrasts his present grief with past happiness, beginning

> So cruel a prison how could betide, alas,
>   As proud Windsor, where I, in lust and joy,
> With a king's son my childish years did pass,
>   In greater feast than Priam's sons of Troy.

With affection and humour the poet pictures the castle life of the two young men about court. No doubt time was spent with their books as well, but the poem suggests that their energies were devoted to athletic competition, as they strove to gain the favours of the "ladies bright of hue".

There is a nice touch when Surrey ruefully notes that keeping an eye on a maiden rather than the ball on the tennis court resulted in missed shots. In friendly rivalry they engaged in jousts on the "gravelled grounds" of the tilting yard, each bearing the sleeve of the chosen beloved on their helmets. They raced each other in the meadows, and in the "wild forest" chased the hart (a pun is clearly intended). Surrey ends his poem with the ironic thought that the misery of his enforced stay at Windsor is only eased by the larger unhappiness at the loss of his friend:

Thus I alone, where all my freedom grew,
In prison pine with bondage and restraint,

And with remembrance of the greater grief,
To banish the less I find my chief relief.

In fact Surrey spent only a few weeks confined at the Castle (and he wasn't languishing in a dungeon but merely forbidden to leave the grounds), and he was back in favour when the court celebrated the birth of Henry's son, Edward. Soon afterwards Jane died and Henry's marital career continued, as did the see-saw fortunes of the Howards, peaking again when he made his fifth marriage to the foolish and flighty Katherine Howard, but tumbling once more when she was executed for adultery.

Though Henry found a sixth bride there was little hope of more children, so anticipating Henry's death and the reign of a young boy, the Howards and Seymours jockeyed for power. At the end of 1547, when the King lay on his death-bed, the faction led by Edward Seymour (now Earl of Hertford) brought charges against Surrey that he had committed high treason by including in his own coat of arms those of King Edward the Confessor—to which he was legally entitled. This, it was alleged, showed his own ambition for the crown. The death warrant was stamped with a wooden signature, but the old tyrant probably did approve of the execution of a man he once loved like a son. Surrey went to the block just nine days before Henry himself died (and was buried in St George's Chapel beside Jane Seymour). Surrey's homes, possessions and even clothing were looted by Hertford, the new king's "Lord Protector". The courtier-poet's reputation lived on however, long after Hertford himself became the victim of plotting, and perished likewise by the executioner's axe.

> What tempest, I trow, threw this whale, with so many tuns of oil in his belly, ashore at Windsor?

Mistress Ford is speaking in Shakespeare's play *The Merry Wives of Windsor*, during which Sir John Falstaff—"two yards and more" around the waist—gets his come-uppance from her and the other merry wife, Mistress Page. The play is a light-hearted comedy and Falstaff is no great nobleman playing a dangerous game of power, but because of his status as a knight he thinks the women will find him irresistible. The sin for which Shakespeare shows him brought low is still that of pride in rank.

Legend has it that *The Merry Wives* was written in response to Queen Elizabeth I's desire to see "Sir John in love", following the two parts of *Henry IV* in which he appears. These are serious plays concerned with attempts by contentious nobles to seize power, but the tone is lightened by the inclusion of fat Falstaff and his cronies. *The Merry Wives* became equally popular, and when it was first printed in 1602 the title page announced that "it hath bene divers times Acted by the right Honourable my Lord Chamberlaines servants. Both before her Maiestie, and elsewhere" (the theatrical company with which Shakespeare worked was the Lord Chamberlain's Men). Exactly a century later it was written of the play that it

> pleas'd one of the greatest Queens that ever was in the World...This comedy was written at her Command, and by her direction, and she was so eager to see it Acted, that she commanded it to be finished in fourteen days; and was afterwards, as Tradition tells us, very well pleas'd at the Representation.

The other tradition of the play is that it was first performed in the Chapter Library of the Castle during Garter celebrations. A convincing case has been made in recent times that the play was commissioned for and first performed at the Garter Feast of 23 April 1597; this preceded by a month the actual installation of new knights at St George's Chapel, one of whom that year was Lord Henry Hunsdon, the very Lord Chamberlain who was the players' patron. Supporting evidence is found at the end of the play where Mistress Quickly, disguised as the Fairy Queen, appears in Windsor Great Park and tells her "fairies" that they must prepare Windsor Castle for the ceremony, cleaning the stalls and coats of arms in the Chapel. Nightly they must sing and dance on the greensward, creating a fairy circle "Like to the Garter's compass", and write the motto " Honi soit qui mal y pense"

A performance of The Merry Wives *before Queen Elizabeth I at Windsor Castle, as pictured in Charles Knight's pictorial biography of Shakespeare of 1843*

> In em'rald tufts, flowers purple, blue, and white,
> Like sapphire, pearl, and rich embroidery
> Buckled below fair knighthood's bending knee.

Unfortunately, if this historical dating is correct, the first performance of *The Merry Wives* cannot have been at the Castle, for the Garter Feast was held at Whitehall that year.

It may well be, however, since the play became a favourite, that there was a repeat performance at the time of the installation. Hunsdon is said to have ridden to this with a train of three hundred men dressed in his livery of orange taffeta; other noble lords were there with their splendidly-dressed retinues, so the occasion must have provided a fine sight for the real-life Fords and Pages of Windsor.

Whatever the circumstances of performance, we can feel sure from the nature of the play that Shakespeare himself was familiar with the town. The references to places are extraordinarily specific, more so than for any other play. Characters scurry to and fro between Windsor itself, Eton, Datchet,

Frogmore, Old Windsor and the Park; local publisher Charles Knight spent time last century tracking the movements of characters from place to place, concluding that the dramatist had a clear and accurate idea of local geography.

Perhaps Shakespeare even stayed at the Garter Inn where he has Falstaff putting up. We know that the Garter Inn adjoined the White Hart Inn and was almost opposite Castle Hill, though we don't know its landlord then, which is a pity as Shakespeare makes the good-humoured "Host" a character in the play. Were the sharp-witted wives and their husbands modelled on anyone in particular? Both Ford and Page are names found in Windsor records. A tradition held that the Ford house was amongst those which used to be directly under the Castle walls, and almost opposite the Garter Inn. Fictional or not, the group of characters—local business men, a justice from Gloucestershire and his cousin the schoolmaster, a French physician and a Welsh parson—suggest a prosperous, cosmopolitan town with a thriving middle class: it is Page's and Ford's wealth that Falstaff has his eye on in his amorous attempts on their wives.

The best-known episode in the play is the one where Falstaff, fearful of discovery by Mistress Ford's jealous husband, is persuaded to hide in a buck basket (that is a laundry basket for the "buck" or bleaching wash). "Foul linen"—smelly stockings, dirty shirts and smocks, and greasy napkins—is packed on top of the great-bellied knight, and the basket carried off by Mistress Ford's servants. She instructs them to take it to the "whitsters [*whiteners*] in Datchet Mead, and there empty it in the muddy ditch close by

Washing, drying and bleaching in a buck wash

Herne's Oak, from Harrison Ainsworth's Windsor Castle *of 1843*

the Thames side''. The Mead was the flat area below the Castle where linen could be spread out to bleach and the route was along Datchet Lane, as the unfortunate knight testifies when he returns dripping wet to the inn. He calls for a quart of ale, complaining of being thrown into the Thames ''like a barrow of butcher's offal''—which gives us good insight into Elizabethan waste disposal.

Falstaff hasn't learnt his lesson though, and he is tricked twice more before he does. On the final occasion the wives talk him into disguising himself as the legendary Herne the Hunter and meeting them at midnight at his oak-tree. There the former keeper of the Forest is said to appear with horns on his head, shaking a chain and casting evil spells on the trees and cattle. Gullible Sir John fastens on a pair of horns and transforms himself into ''a Windsor stag, and the fattest, I think, i'th'forest''. But waiting to ambush him at the oak is a ''fairy'' band; the wives run away in mock terror and the fairies set upon him, pinching him and burning him with their tapers. Pulling off his deer disguise Falstaff ruefully admits that he has instead been made ''an ass''.

Much has been written about both the legend of Herne the Hunter and his oak. Shakespeare's is the first reference in print to a legend which presumably he picked up from local sources: sceptics have suggested that he made the story up, but it seems to fit a pattern in European mythology of hauntings by wild huntsmen. Identification of Herne's Oak, and the "pit" nearby where the ambushers wait, have aroused a great deal of argument over the centuries: the strongest claim for the oak-tree seems to have been for one which died and was felled in the reign of George III. But there are still plenty of old oaks in the Park under whose boughs Shakespeare could have sat. It's quite reasonable to imagine him as a visitor in Windsor, enjoying the hospitality of the Garter Inn, and perhaps quaffing its good ale after a long walk taken through the fields before returning "from Frogmore, over the stile".

When the old Queen, the last Tudor monarch, died in 1603 her cousin King James VI of Scotland inherited the throne as James I of England. Luckily Shakespeare and his company found favour and came directly under James's patronage as the King's Men. But his contemporary, Sir Walter Ralegh, the proud young favourite of Queen Elizabeth's last years, was not so lucky: he was arrested, condemned for treason and sent to the Tower.

Ralegh's position with the old Queen made James distrust him long before he came to England, though since both were men of literary taste that might have brought them together. Both wrote poetry, Ralegh celebrating in verse his admiration of "Cynthia" (the Queen), while in the tradition of his ancestor, James I of Scotland, King James had produced volumes of poetry in his native kingdom (one was titled *His Majesties Poeticall Exercises at Vacant Houres*, but after becoming King of England he wrote no more, presumably no longer having vacant hours). He also wrote a pamphlet on witchcraft called *Daemonologie*, said to have influenced Shakespeare's *Macbeth*, and a year after his accession published his *Counterblaste to Tobacco*, in which he attacked the new leisure activity of smoking as

> a custom loathsome to the eye, hateful to the nose, harmful to the brain, dangerous to the lungs, and in the black, stinking fume thereof, nearest resembling the horrible Stygian smoke of the pit that is bottomless.

James' objection to pipe smoking may have coloured his feelings about Ralegh who was an inveterate smoker.

Ralegh's fame rested on his seafaring exploits against the Spanish and as a coloniser and explorer of the New World, hunting for gold from the legendary South American mines, or seizing it pirate-fashion from the Spanish. Obsessed with hatred of the Spanish he could not appreciate that James wanted peace, and seems not to have been aware of a vicious campaign being waged with James against him (one of its leaders being the Earl of Surrey's son).

Ironically Ralegh's last moments of freedom before his arrest were spent on the North Terrace of Windsor Castle which Elizabeth had created, and where he had strutted in days when his enemies spoke of him as the "uncrowned king of England". Only three months after the accession, Ralegh was waiting on the Terrace one July day, expecting to follow the King's hunt (James had a passion for hunting and quickly made Windsor a favourite amongst the royal palaces), when he was ordered to remain behind to be questioned about an alleged plot against the King. Lack of evidence did not prevent a trial, and a verdict of guilty being brought in.

In the Tower Ralegh turned to writing again, working at an ambitious *History of the World*. But he was still obsessed with South American gold, and after thirteen years in captivity was allowed by James to organise another expedition. It was a disastrous failure, involving Ralegh in an attack on the Spanish which James had expressly forbidden. On his return he was rearrested, sent back to the Tower, and finally executed under the treason verdict from fifteen years earlier. His bravery on the scaffold where he felt the sharp edge of the axe and smilingly declared that "This is that that will cure all sorrows", created much sympathy for him and resentment against James. While it would be exaggerating to say that James' decision that Ralegh should lose his head led directly to his successor, Charles I, losing his, the execution helped to set in motion the catastrophic turn of Fortune's wheel for the second Stuart king.

CHAPTER THREE

Diarists

Samuel Pepys (1633-1703), John Evelyn (1620-1706)

Samuel Pepys

WHEN THE DIARIST Samuel Pepys visited Windsor Castle on 26 February 1666 he enthusiastically pronounced it "the most romantique castle that is in the world", creating a phrase which has been repeated time and time again since. Yet whatever their overall truth it is odd that Pepys should have used those words then, for the most recent drama to have been played out within the Castle walls was the imprisonment before execution of King Charles I, followed by the return of his decapitated body for unceremonious burial in the Chapel. Charles II was restored to the throne in 1660, by which time the Castle had fallen into decay. Four years after Pepys' visit the diarist John Evelyn more soberly wrote of its "exceedingly ragged and ruinous" state.

Pepys and the older Evelyn knew each other well, yet were never aware that they were both diarists. Neither man wrote for other eyes to see, indeed Pepys used a disguising shorthand and hid his most intimate revelations further behind a strange polyglot language of his own devising. Yet once deciphered, his diaries proved to offer an extraordinarily vivid, lively account of London life in the 1660s. Since the decade brought a series of very dramatic events—the Restoration, the Plague, the Great Fire of London, the sea war with the Dutch—Pepys' diaries also provide day-to-day accounts of history as it was being made.

His first visit to Windsor was unfortunately as a bringer of bad news. Pepys worked for the Navy Board and it was his duty in August 1665, in the year of the plague, to visit Sir George Carteret, Treasurer of the Navy, to tell him of a reverse the fleet had suffered at the hands of the Dutch. Sir George lived at Cranbourne Lodge in Windsor Great Park (where only the Tower remains). He had been granted the Lodge a couple of years earlier and was busy rebuilding it.

Pepys hired a guide and horses from a London post-house and rode to another at Hounslow (where, having an eye for a pretty face, he noted a little girl called Betty Gysby "which, if she lives, will make a great beauty"). From there he rode to Staines and hired a guide to take him through Windsor forest. But by this time it was dark and the guide lost his way. Pepys himself got them back on track, thankful for the skills he'd acquired from studying the movements of the moon. Finally he reached the Lodge

> where in the dark I perceive an old house new-building with a great deal of Rubbish, and was fain to go up a ladder to Sir G. Carteret's chamber. And there in his bed I sat down and told him all my bad news, which troubled him mightily, but yet we were merry and made the best of it; and being myself weary, did take leave... So to sleep –being very well but weary, and the better by having carried with me a bottle of strong water–whereof now and then a sip did me good.

"Strong water", as can be guessed, was spirits. Next day Pepys looked around him and found Cranbourne to be

> a very noble seat, in a noble forest, with the noblest prospect toward Windsor and round about over many Countys that can be desired.

But he qualified his rapture by saying that it was "otherwise a very melancholy place and little variety save only Trees".

He hoped to visit the Castle, but Sir George wanted him to return at once, so after eating "a bit off the spit" he rode directly to the riverside at Brentford. There, as the tide was out and it was Sunday, he went to church and listened to "a dull sermon". In the evening he hired a boat and reached the city after dark, his waterman very fearful of the plague:

> Thence with a lanthorn, in great fear of meeting of dead corses carrying to be buried; but blessed be God, met none... So got safe home about 10 o'clock, my people not all a-bed; and after supper, I weary to bed.

It had been an eventful forty-eight hours.

Cranbourne Tower

The following February Pepys got his chance to visit Windsor and to take his wife with him. (He had married a girl much younger than himself, the fifteen-year-old daughter of Huguenot refugees, Elizabeth St Michel, in 1655: he did not always treat her well, and was repeatedly unfaithful to her.) He hired a coach and four, and took servants with him. It must have been especially exciting for Mrs Pepys, and he recorded that she got up between three and four o'clock in the morning to dress herself for the occasion. They started at six and by eleven had reached Cranbourne, where Pepys was engaged to meet the Earl of Sandwich (a naval commander and diplomat, his relation and patron). After dinner Pepys walked with the Earl in the park and engaged in political talk, but the serious mood disappeared indoors. Lady Carteret invited him to stay the night and when she went away with the Earl

> I with the young ladies and gentlemen, who played on the guitarr and mighty merry, and anon to supper; and then my Lord going away to write, the young gentlemen to flinging of cushions and other mad sports.

Was Mrs Pepys left out of the fun? Around midnight the two of them retired to a "passage-room" to bed, but the young people's high jinks seem to have continued for he complains of sleeping badly because of the noise.

Next morning they set out for Windsor. It was to be a splendid day: Pepys, treated at his parting from the nobility at Cranbourne with much "love and kindness", and feeling like a lord in his coach and four, thought himself to be "in the happiest occasion a man can be". It is no wonder that he saw the Castle through a rosy glow.

They were set down at Shakespeare's old Garter Inn (which was to be burnt to the ground fifteen years later). Pepys then sent for an acquaintance, Dr William Childs, who took them to St George's Chapel and before showing them round gave them cushions to sit on while the choir sang a special anthem and service, just for them. The visit to the Castle followed, where all amazed and delighted:

> But Lord, the prospect that is in the balcone in the Queen's lodgings, and the tarrace and walk, are strange things to consider, being the best in the world, sure.

It is pleasing to note that Pepys felt that his wife's pleasure in the occasion added to his own satisfaction. But she was left in the coach when, after dining at the inn with the Doctor, he went on to visit Eton College. This he thought "mighty fine", and he enjoyed the home-brewed College beer too. At length "finely, but sleepy" they set off back home.

Later that year came the apocalyptic Fire of London which devastated most of the city. Pepys was told by Lady Carteret that pieces of burnt paper were blown as far as Cranbourne. He noted with awe that on one piece were written the words "Time is, it is done".

London had to be rebuilt and so, as Evelyn records though Pepys seems not to have noticed, had much of the Castle. It had been used as a prison under Cromwell and had also been taken over by squatters. A parliamentary bill to sell off the Castle and its lands "for ready money" had only narrowly been defeated. After the Restoration the squatters were quickly evicted, but Charles II gave his first attention to restoring St George's Chapel. It had suffered terribly when Cromwell's soldiers had been garrisoned at the Castle; in their puritan zeal they smashed windows and rendered the interior almost unrecognisable. They had also looted the treasures. But by the time Pepys visited it the Knights of the Garter were re-established and the Chapel refurbished.

John Evelyn

John Evelyn's diary—more accurately called memoirs since he wrote events up later from notes rather than from day to day—covers a much longer period of time than Pepys'; he gave up his diary in 1669 when he felt it was over-straining his eyesight. Thus we know from Evelyn that both men were present when on an August evening in 1674 a thousand spectators watched a re-enactment of the siege of Maastricht, recently captured from the French, in the meadows below the Castle Terrace. A model of the fortress had been constructed and it was attacked by a small army, with guns firing and mines exploding. Evelyn found it "realy very divertisant", but one would like to have had some of Pepys' superlatives as well.

Evelyn was a wealthy Royalist who was high in Charles II's favour, and he saw the Castle's gradual transformation from the ragged state to one of rich splendour. In his own day Evelyn was famous for his book *Sylva* about the planting and management of woodlands, published just at the time when landowners, including Charles himself to whom the book was dedicated, were trying to repair the ravages of the Civil War. In 1683 Evelyn noted with satisfaction the newly-created "Avenues to the New-Park, & other Walkes planted with Elmes & limes, and a pretty Canale, & receptacle for fowle". In *Sylva* Evelyn had written of the elm that there is "no tree, whatever, becoming long Walks and Avenues, comparable to this Majestic plant". In 1685 the King created his magnificent Long Walk with elm trees so, though the elms had to be felled earlier this century, we may have Evelyn's influence at least in part to thank for this distinctive feature of Windsor's landscape.

Evelyn was certainly responsible for one of the glories of the Castle refurbishment within, as it was he who discovered Grinling Gibbons, the wood-carver. He relates how he found him

> in an Obscure place, & that by meere accident, as I was walking neere a poore solitary thatched house in a field in our Parish.

He looked in through the window and was amazed to see a young man elaborately carving a copy of a Tintoretto Crucifixion. He asked the price and was told a hundred pounds:

> In good earnest the very frame was worth the mony, there being nothing even in nature so tender, & delicate as the flowers & festoones about it.

When he next saw the King he begged to be allowed to bring the young man to court, but trusting Evelyn's judgement Charles said that he would himself seek him out. Some years later Evelyn saw what had been produced in the Castle and with justifiable pride commented on

> the stupendious, & beyond all description, the incomparable Carving of our Gibbons, who is (without Contraversie) the greatest Master, both for Invention, & rareness of Worke, that the world ever had in any age.

Exaggeration? Most visitors to the Castle would echo the description of Gibbons' work as "incomparable", and rejoice both that the carving was spared by the fire of 1992 and that the diarist paused in his walk, curious enough to look through the window of the "poore thatched house" to see what was going on.

Evelyn also admired the work of the fresco painter Verrio, who had been adorning ceilings in the Castle and whose work he thought would last "as long as those walls last". Unfortunately not all the ceilings were structurally sound and some of the frescos had to be removed when Wyattville restored the state rooms for George IV. One which was lost showed Charles II most inappropriately in the company of Prudence, Temperance and Fortitude. Despite his good relations with the King, Evelyn could not approve of the frivolity of the court and the parade of the King's mistresses.

Even Pepys, no sexual angel himself, disapproved, and he records himself and Evelyn discussing matters once for a couple of hours, "talking of the badness of the government, where nothing but wickedness, and wicked men and women command the King''. Pepys snorted with contempt at an account of the King and his brother drunk at Cranbourne and ''in such a maudlin pickle as never people were''. But with his eye for a pretty face and his love of theatre, he was rather taken with the saucy comedienne Nell Gwyn who was another of Charles' women, established in a house just outside the Castle walls (aristocratic mistresses were bedded within).

After the death of the (officially) childless Charles II, his Catholic brother James II reigned till the Protestant revolution of 1688 drove him from the country. Pepys then resigned his position in the Navy Office and devoted himself to pursuits such as book collection. Though twenty years younger than Evelyn he died first, in 1703, requesting in his will that Evelyn be one of the pall-bearers at his funeral. But Evelyn was unwell and could not be present. In his diary however he paid generous tribute to his old friend, as

> a very worthy, Industrious & curious person... universaly beloved, Hospitable, Generous, Learned in many things, skill'd in Musick, a very greate Cherisher of Learned men, of whom he had the conversation.

Amongst the cherished learned Evelyn himself was certainly one.

CHAPTER FOUR

Travellers

Celia Fiennes (1662-1741),
Daniel Defoe (1660-1731), William Cobbett (1763-1835)

IT MIGHT BE SAID that tourism was invented in the late seventeenth century. Not that people didn't travel around before and enjoy it, but they did so usually for a purpose: travel for travel's sake, travel to broaden the mind, was a new idea. It caught on quickly: by the next century continental travel was well-established and it had become part of a young aristocrat's education to be sent off on the Grand Tour. Our stately homes are full of the treasures with which they returned.

Exploration and discovery of Great Britain also had its attractions. A sense of national pride was developing and there was a desire to know about the country, to chart its landscapes and learn about its peoples. The first book of road maps, called *Britannia* and printed to look like long unfolding scrolls, was published by John Ogilvy in 1675, and encouraged the curious to follow the routes.

Not that the journeys were either easy or safe. Roads were in poor repair and, with increasing enclosure (when land was taken into private ownership and fenced in for farming), many which once had been broad highways had been reduced to narrow tracks. This had in turn made ambush by highwaymen easier: muggings and even murders along the way were commonplace. Maidenhead Thicket was one notorious criminal hangout; in January 1695 alone no fewer than fifty people were held up there. Such difficulties and dangers make even more remarkable the journeys of a woman on her own, Celia Fiennes.

She was born in 1662 just after the Restoration, and was the daughter of a Roundhead colonel and grand-daughter of Viscount Saye and Sele, one of the instigators of the parliamentary revolt against the monarchy. But the family was not persecuted after Charles II's return. Very little is known about Celia's personal life and no portrait of her exists, but being unmarried must have given her the time and independence to travel. For about thirty years from the age of twenty she set off regularly on horseback journeys around the country, riding side-saddle and with only one or two servants in attendance.

Her first journeys were made to visit some of her numerous relatives, but later she undertook much longer pilgrimages. Celia says that she wrote accounts of her journeys for her near relations and not for publication (the manuscripts were first transcribed and published by a family descendant in 1888). She began her travels for reasons of health, but having found herself so thoroughly suited by her experiences she is forth-right in recommending them to all:

> ... if all persons, both Ladies, much more Gentlemen, would spend some of their tyme in Journeys to visit their native Land, and be curious to inform themselves and make observations of the pleasant prospects, good buildings, different produces and manufactures of each place, with the variety of sports and recreations they are adapt to, would be a souveraign remedy to cure or preserve from these epidemick diseases of vapours, should I add Laziness?

Celia is aware that she writes as she would speak: "most I converse with knows both the freedom and easyness I speak and write as well as my deffect in all". But the lack of grammatical structure and stylistic embellishment does not seem a defect. Her enthusiasms and strictures, piled on top of each other with little punctuation, have spontaneity and charm. We travel with her and gather impressions just as they catch her eye, as if in running commentary.

Celia Fiennes
(as imagined by Michael Bayley)

Her most ambitious or "Great Journey" was made in 1698, during the reign of William III (the Dutch king who had married James II's protestant daughter Mary II with whom he ruled jointly till her death in 1694). This took her first from London to East Anglia, then across country to Cheshire and into Wales, back over the sands of Dee and up into the Lake District, then over the Scottish border, before turning south to Newcastle and a steady progression down through England all the way to Land's End. Last stop on her return was a visit to Windsor and Eton.

It had been raining solidly for two days and her route from Bagshot was hard going through the heavy clay and deep puddles. Undaunted however, she began her sightseeing in Windsor at once, starting with St George's Chapel. A very precise and practical observer, her beady eye missing nothing, she catalogues every tomb and statue, telling us exactly how many Garter Knights there are, how many singing men and what they're paid. She ends in admiration of the roof of the choir

> which is very curious carv'd stone and soe thinn to the leads one might grasp it between thumb and finger and yet so well fixt as to be very strong.

Next she is off up the hundred and twenty steps to the Round Tower, where she passes rapidly through the Guard room, a dining room, drawing-room and two bed chambers—pausing a moment, her domestic eye caught by the new mode half bedstead in one, "dimity with fine shades of worstead works well made up", and in the other the same kind of bed "but that is a fine Indian quilting and embroidery of silk"—before hurrying up "as many stepps more" to the leads, where she can stop and take a long look around at the huge prospect of forest and countryside as far as Kensington and Shooters Hill. Below her "the town of Winsor looked very well" with noblemen's houses and fine gardens and the Long Walk stretching into the Forest, while in the other direction she sees "the river Thames which twists and turns it self round the meddowes and grounds". Finally she looks directly down and sees that

> ...in the walls grows the best maiden haire, both white and black, which is an herb much esteemed for coughs and to put into drinks for consumptions.

Then she goes for a more leisurely look round the Castle, noting all the new works, like the Verrio frescos and the work of Gibbons, the "masterpiece of all such work both in figures fruitages beasts birds flowers all sorts, soe thinn the wood and all white natural wood without varnish". But with her Puritan background she is less impressed with the elaborate throne of state created to give audience to the French Ambassador, though sniffily acknowledging that

> some of these foolerys are requisite sometymes to create admiration and regard to keep up the state of a kingdom and nation.

Out from the Castle and into the street, where she sees again that "Winsor town lookes well, the streets large the Market Cross on stone pillars and a large Hall on the top'' (the Guildhall, completed by Sir Christopher Wren just ten years earlier). Then down to the river and across the bridge for a quick look and head count at Eton before seeking the Datchet ferry, riding along ''in sight of the Castle on this side which is all the Kings and Queens appartments and lookes very noble''. Finally via Colnbrook and Hounslow Heath

> ...and so to London; here ends my Long Journey this summer, in which I had but 3 dayes of wet except some refreshing showers sometymes... in all which way and tyme I desire with thankfullness to own the good providence of God protecting me from all hazard and dangerous accident.

Celia came back to Windsor a few years later as part of a shorter journey in the reign of Queen Anne, and described what was new or omitted from her first description. Near the south terrace of the Castle the Queen had purchased a small house for herself and her husband, Prince George, in preference to living within the Castle; Celia went to have a look around this ''little box'' (Horace Walpole was later to describe it more elegantly as the ''footstool'' of the Castle). She left no door handle unturned in her exploration: it is amazing what liberty visitors then had to poke and pry around. Investigating a closet in Prince George's dressing room she was impressed to find a flush toilet, ''a little place with a seat of easement of marble with sluces of water to wash all down''. The Queen's room above she found locked, but examination of a waiting-room to one side revealed more such ''marble seats of easement'', while on the other was a ''little closet with the tea equipage''. One feels she should have asked for a cup of tea and a chance to use the facilities.

On this occasion Celia must have travelled by coach, as afterwards she drove into Windsor Forest to watch a sort of marathon race. It was between two footmen, one English one Scots. A circular course of nearly four miles had been created and the men were to run round it for twenty-two miles, the distance between Charing Cross and Windsor Cross (the market cross found roughly where Queen Victoria's statue is today)—''that was five times quite round and so farre as made up the odd miles''. They completed it in two and a half hours, which sounds good going, and there was an exciting finish: the Englishman got the lead in the second round and kept it up for all five rounds, but then

> ...the Scotch-man came up to him and got before him to the post; the Englishman fell down within a few yeards of the post; many hundred pounds were won and lost about it, they ran both very neatly but my

> judgment gave it the Scotch man because he seem'd to save himself to the last push.

It was clearly a good piece of tactical running.

Celia Fiennes died in 1741. She had no children, but one of her family descendants is Sir Ranulph Fiennes, the present-day explorer (who was born in the Princess Christian Nursing Home in Windsor): adventure must be in the Fiennes blood.

Daniel Defoe was another round-Britain traveller. He is best known today as a novelist, creator of the fictional adventurer Robinson Crusoe, but he could turn his hand to almost any kind of writing and produced over five hundred different works. One of them, *A Tour through the Whole Island of Great Britain*, was published in 1724, after he had made a number of journeys to learn what he could about the nation's industry and economy.

Defoe likewise visited Windsor, as part of a journey along the Thames valley. His principal interest was in the busy trading going on up and down river to London: when roads were poor, navigable rivers were of vital importance for the distribution of goods. He marvels at the great flow of commerce, recording how at Reading barges bring "coals, salt, grocery wares, tobacco, oyls, and all heavy goods", and carry back "very great quantities of malt, and meal". Corn mills and paper mills lined the tributary river Loddon nearby; Marlow is described as a "town of very great embarkation", while Bisham had mills for brass kettle and pan making, another for the production of thimbles—a much-needed item then—and another for pressing oil from rape and flax seed. Quantities of beech wood were transported down river from the Buckinghamshire woodlands, sustaining the great city of London in its need for carts, furniture and building material. Henley and Maidenhead were two other busy little commercial stations.

But when Defoe comes to Windsor he says he must

> leave talking of trade, river, navigation, meal, and malt, and describe the most beautiful, and most pleasantly situated castle, and royal palace, in the whole isle of Britain.

He writes enthusiastically and at length about the Castle, using phrases like "magnificent work", "noble walk", "lofty terrace". It's a pity though that

Windsor when the Thames was busy with transport of people and heavy goods

he didn't find more to say about the town itself other than that it has a wooden bridge (all the bridges from London to Oxford were made of wood, he tells us, for the convenience of the barges): we know that in fact Windsor was as busy with trade as anywhere else on the river, with coal the principal cargo unloaded on its wharves, and beer from the Windsor Brewery taken on board the barges. Nevertheless Defoe makes us aware of the vital nature of the traffic which flowed up and down the river, busy as a motorway today in shifting the nation's goods, but quietly, steadily, and without pollution. As he looks out from the windows of the castle over the north terrace, he sees

> part of the finest, and richest, vale in the world...The river, with a winding, and beautiful stream, gliding gently through the middle of it, and inriching by its navigation, both the land and the people on every side.

If William Cobbett were alive today he would surely be leading the conservation, anti-pollution lobby, thundering protest at the theft of good agricultural land for motorways, commuter housing estates and out-of-town supermarkets. A hundred years after Defoe he too travelled round Great Britain in a series of journeys, but in his case it was to examine the state of rural England, which he believed was being led into decline by misguided government policies. His observations were published in the *Political Register*, a weekly journal which he founded and made a mouthpiece for a working-class point of view. He would be amazed to know that his day-to-day journalism, published under the title *Rural Rides*, is now regarded as part of our literary heritage.

Cobbett was nearly sixty when he started his rides. He had been born of farming stock at Farnham in Surrey and had led a varied and enterprising life. For a while he was a soldier (during which time he taught himself to read and write); later he lived for some years in America, where he began his career in political journalism, coming to the defence of his native land against those who attacked it there. On his return home a gratified British government offered him the chance to run a government-controlled paper. Though proud to have risen so high, he would not allow himself to become politically chained, and he soon became a thorn in the flesh of the THING, his word and capitals for what we would call the establishment.

In his writings Cobbett pulls no punches and he can be appallingly prejudiced and pig-headed, but his rage was an honest anger at poverty and injustice observed at first hand. Where Defoe marvelled at how the great city of London was supported by the country's industries, Cobbett railed at the city's "stock-jobbers and tax-eaters" growing rich at the expense of old agricultural communities. For him London was "the Great Wen", a festering sore. But he isn't just a polemicist: his *Rural Rides* are also full of sensitive observations of nature, enjoyment of good food or appreciation of a pretty face, often offered with engaging inconsequence.

In October 1822 he set off on a series of rides through Hampshire, Berkshire, Surrey and Sussex. His forthright style is well-illustrated by his entry for 31 October:

> Set off at daylight and got to Kensington about noon. On leaving Oakingham [Wokingham] for London, you get upon what is called Windsor Forest; that is to say, upon as bleak, as barren, and as villainous a heath as ever man set his eyes on.

Some years earlier Parliament had allowed the enclosure of heaths and wastelands not already in private ownership, a scandalous proceeding to Cobbett who believed that the countryside had thus been depopulated and was "wasting away". He was an early objector to commuters who worked in the city and wanted fancy houses and pretty gardens to come home to:

> As to this rascally heath, that which has ornamented it has brought misery on millions. The spot is not distant from the stock-jobbing crew. The roads to it are level. They are smooth. The wretches can go to it from the 'Change [Exchange] without any danger to their rascally necks.

Cobbett had a bee in his bonnet about this kind of agricultural decline, claiming without evidence that at Sunninghill the "tax-eaters" who had made grounds and gardens there "have beggared twenty agricultural villages and hamlets".

A few days later he resumed his journey, setting off from Egham. It was now November, and the morning chilly:

> Started at day-break in a hazy frost, for Reading. The horses' manes and ears covered with the hoar before we got across Windsor Park.

Again he repeats that the soil hereabouts is "blackguard", but the roads are good, "such as might have been made by Solomon". Defoe had found the parks about Windsor "very agreeable...open for riding, hunting, and taking the air for any gentlemen that please", but Cobbett could not enjoy the easy ride without reflecting that this paradise of "pretty roads with edgings cut to line" must be at the expense of labourers' clothes and food.

Happily, when he got to Binfield he was able to enjoy his breakfast at "a very nice country inn called the Stag and Hounds", without any uncomfortable reflection that his full belly might mean another's empty one.

Unlike Fiennes and Defoe, Cobbett did not visit Windsor itself. He would not necessarily have been abusive: a few months earlier he had found High Wycombe "a very fine and very clean market town". (He also cast his farmer's eye over the female livestock and found the girls of the town not as good-looking as those of Sussex, but "like the girls of America, and that is saying quite as much as any reasonable woman can expect or wish for"). If he had been to Windsor he'd hardly have resisted having a dig at the reigning monarch George IV, whose Brighton Pavilion he'd described as a square box with five Norfolk turnips on top, nor a swipe against his least favourite king, buried in the Chapel, that "ferocious tyrant" and "ruffian" Henry VIII.

Defoe and Cobbett offer contrasting pictures of the area. For Defoe it is busily prosperous, for Cobbett wretchedly declined. A hundred years had brought change: Defoe's journey coincided with a period of economic confidence, Cobbett's with a time of great agricultural depression following the Napoleonic Wars. But temperament and political persuasion played their parts also, Defoe's view being perhaps too rose-tinted, Cobbett's too blinkered. If they could have time-travelled to each others' ages, would they have altered their perspectives at all?

Thames Street in the early nineteenth century, showing the old Curfew Tower and buildings lining the ditch

CHAPTER FIVE

Voices for Peace

Jonathan Swift (1667-1745), Alexander Pope (1688-1744)

Jonathan Swift

"WINDSOR IS A delicious situation, but the town is scoundrel." So wrote the Irish clergyman Dr Jonathan Swift, future author of *Gulliver's Travels*, when he arrived in July 1711 in the reign of Queen Anne. The town stands condemned without charge, as Swift doesn't explain his criticism, but just as Pepys' description of the Castle as "romantic" has been quoted repeatedly, so has Swift's denigration of the town as "scoundrel".

What were the grounds of his objection? Not much more than a decade earlier Celia Fiennes had commented favourably on Windsor with its handsome gentlemen's houses and gardens, seen as she looked towards the Long Walk from the top of the Castle keep. But in the other direction she might have noted the overcrowded insanitary slums of an area bordered by Peascod Street, Thames Street and the river, and it is assumed that it was these mean streets which Swift was condemning. Conditions in them were made worse by stinking rubbish, despite bye-laws forbidding Windsor citizens to keep pigs or to make dunghills in the street, or to throw out rotting fish, offal, or vegetable refuse. In his poem 'A City Shower' Swift describes the effects of a deluge of rain on London streets, and there is no reason to suppose that Windsor was any different:

Sweepings from butchers' stalls, dung, guts, and blood,
Drown'd puppies, stinking sprats, all drench'd in mud,
Dead cats and turnip-tops come tumbling down the flood.

The problems of refuse and sanitation were to get much worse as the century went on.

But Swift had come to Windsor for the Castle, to make himself known in court circles in the hope of church preferment. Born and educated in Ireland he was vicar of an Irish living, but he hoped to win the Queen's favour and be rewarded by an English deanery. In the political "party" system which had established itself, he was introduced at court by the chief Tory ministers; he had allied himself to them because of their desire to make peace with France after a long war. Swift hated war and was willing to desert his previous Whig friends and become a Tory pamphleteer for peace.

On his first visit to Windsor Swift stayed for some time in lodgings at the Castle; over the next couple of years he sometimes lodged, sometimes travelled down for the day in the coach of Robert Harley, the Treasurer and chief minister. At other times he made the three-hour journey with Secretary of State Henry St John. In a letter he describes himself as being "tosticated" to and from Windsor, but it was undoubtedly gratifying to be closeted thus with the great men of state.

His lodgings, at least on one occasion, had a fine view of Eton and the Thames, and Swift wished they belonged to him. But his domestic life was in general far from smooth because of his wayward Irish servant Patrick, who caused a deal of trouble. He would forget to do the packing, was frequently drunk, and on one occasion managed to go off with the key to their lodgings, leaving his master to cool his heels for several hours in the Cloisters. When he finally returned Swift gave him "two or three swinging cuffs on the ear", but in pulling and punching his servant about the master managed to strain his thumb and suffered pain himself for days.

During the three years of visits to Windsor Swift wrote a kind of daily journal, or rather a series of letters, to a woman in Ireland he called "Stella" (her real name was Esther Johnson), so we can get a picture of his life on the fringes of the court. Because of his literary reputation he felt a degree of confidence and wrote that he was "so proud that I make all the lords come up to me". It was less gratifying to hear from his political friends that they had been talking of him to the Queen, and "she said, she had never heard of me".

Queen Anne was forty-six years old at this time but, grossly fat and suffering from gout and dropsy, she looked much older and had to be carried around in a chair. Much of her ill-health stemmed from the numerous pregnancies she'd undergone in pursuit of an heir: she bore no fewer than eighteen babies, but the only one to live any length of time died at the age of eleven. Depressed and unwell as she was, it is not surprising that the picture Swift gives of a reception at the Castle is one of paralysing dullness:

> There was a drawing-room at Court; but so few company, that the queen sent for us into her bed-chamber, where we made our bows, and stood about twenty of us round the room, while she looked at us round with her fan in her mouth, and once a minute said about three words to some that were nearest her, and then she was told dinner was ready, and went out.

There was one activity, however, sure to rouse the Queen from lethargy: Anne was a passionate huntress. She had had a special one-horse, one-seater hunting chariot designed for her in which she careered around the Great Park on roads she had had laid down for the purpose. "She drives furiously, like Jehu, and is a mighty hunter, like Nimrod," wrote Swift. Just the day before his dull reception she had covered forty miles in her chariot and was probably very tired.

Swift was not himself an enthusiastic horseman, but a couple of days later he borrowed a horse, and rode out with Dr Arbuthnot, the Queen's physician, to see the park. They went as far as Ascot, to "a place they have made for a famous horse-race tomorrow", and fell in with a Miss Forester. It was not a very enjoyable ride however. Swift was wearied by his "trotting mettlesome horse", and found Miss Forester irritating, "a silly true maid of honour", dressed in the newly-fashionable "male" attire for women on horseback, at least for the upper half. Miss Forester doffed her hat like a man as the Queen went by. Swift felt the effects of his uncomfortable ride for the next three days, and missed the historic inauguration of racing at Ascot on the following day, 11 August 1711. He was much happier walking in the Park, and did so as often as possible, particularly admiring the Long Walk, "the finest avenue I ever saw". It was Queen Anne who created the road between its double rows of elms along which Swift then, and countless Windsorians and tourists since, have sauntered.

On one occasion he was accompanied there on a walk by a young woman, Esther Vanhomrigh. Swift's relationships with his two Esthers, "Stella" of the *Journals* and "Vanessa" as she appears in his literary writings, are enigmatic. He had known Stella as a child and contributed to her education; when she died in 1728 he was desolate as any widower. The letters in journal form which he wrote to her during his London and Windsor years are full of intimate expression: "Presto [Swift] is so silly to-night; yes he be; but Presto loves MD dearly, as hope saved," he writes from his bed at Windsor. Yet it seems that they were only ever verbal lovers, and to complicate matters MD [my dears?] stands not just for Stella, but also for her older companion Rebecca Dingley, to whom for propriety's sake the correspondence was addressed.

Not surprisingly Swift was reticent in telling Stella about Vanessa, daughter of a widow who entertained Swift in London and who may have hoped herself to become Mrs Swift. Stella is told that from Windsor "I have sent a noble haunch of venison this afternoon to Mrs Vanhomrigh; I wish you had it, sirrahs", but it is only his account books which make clear how frequently he dined at her house. Tragically Swift became a passion for Vanessa while he himself settled for a teasing relationship, charted again by language which alternately fanned the flames and damped them down. When

Windsor's Guildhall, completed in 1690

he left England for Ireland she followed him, half encouraged to do so, but was thereafter avoided by him.

From 1711 to 1713 Swift had waited, "tosticating" between the capital and the Castle, for church preferment. But though the Queen once sent to Kensington for some of her preserved ginger, thought likely to help him when he suffered a vomiting illness at Windsor, news of some more substantial gift never came. He wrote to Stella: "If I had not a spirit naturally chearfull, I should be very discontented at a thousand things". He never realised that as far as Queen Anne was concerned nothing was ever going to materialise for him. He had blotted his copybook irrevocably when he maligned her favourite Lady of the Bedchamber, the Duchess of Somerset.

For Anne it was important to have women she loved close to her, but it was a source of fury to her Tory ministers that the Duchess of Somerset had her ear as no-one else. The Duke of Somerset was a Whig, set against the desired peace with France, and through his wife it was thought he was influencing the Queen. At Christmas 1711 Swift published 'The Windsor Prophecy', a verse lampoon which purported to be printed from an ancient parchment discovered in a lead coffer when a grave was dug in the Cloisters. It was a crude attack on the Duchess, unjustly using a tragic event from her past.

In an age when girls born into noble families were marriage fodder, Elizabeth Percy, daughter of the Duke of Northumberland, was already a widow when she was married at fourteen to Thomas Thynne of Longleat. Shortly afterwards he was murdered by a jealous suitor, the Count von Königsmark. Three months later she was married for the third time to the Duke of Somerset. It was a dramatic history, but hardly her fault. The references in Swift's poem are obvious—the Duchess was noted for her red hair:

> ... dear Englond, if ought I understond,
> Beware of Carrots from Northumberland.
> Carrots sown Thyn a deep root may get,
> If so be they are in Sommer set:
> Their Conyngs mark thou, for I have been told,
> They assassine when young and Poison when old.
> Root out these Carrots, O Thou, whose Name
> Is backwards and forwards always the same.

The name was Anna but, like a later queen, she was not amused. She determined that Swift would receive no favours from her.

Yet Swift did get his Deanery, though not an English one. In the spring of 1713, as peace was finally ratified, he became Dean of St Patrick's in Dublin, never realising that it had only come about because this Deanery was in the gift of the Lord Lieutenant of Ireland and not the Queen. Henceforth it was in Ireland that Swift's destiny was shaped, and for Ireland that his powerful voice was raised in protest at English injustice and neglect.

Alexander Pope

Just a month before Doctor became Dean Swift, he closed a letter to Stella with the words "Mr Pope has publishd a fine Poem calld Windsor Forest; read it". He had not at the time met Alexander Pope; later the two men became close friends.

'Windsor Forest' is a poem which Swift would have admired for its dual celebration of the parkland which he had grown to love, and the coming peace. But in writing it Pope was adding new wine to an old bottle, for the bulk had been composed when he was only fifteen, living at Binfield on the fringes of Windsor Forest. His father, a linen merchant, had moved to a small red-brick house on the edge of the village to escape the prejudice against the family's Roman Catholic religion which they had encountered in London. There he cultivated his garden and acquired a reputation for enormous "Hartichokes", while his son explored the neighbouring countryside with his spaniel dog (was it called Bounce? all his later dogs were). The poet regarded his childhood in Windsor Forest as the happiest time of his life, even though he began then to suffer from the tuberculosis of the spine which left him a hunch-backed cripple, only four and a half feet tall.

Pope loved the trees of the Forest: a beech grove near the house became known as Pope's Grove and a carving on one of the trees, "Here Pope sung", was carefully renewed until the tree blew down in 1825. Maybe it was under its boughs that the first part of 'Windsor Forest' was written. Perhaps a little too mannered for modern tastes, owing much to classical models, it is nevertheless remarkable writing for a fifteen-year-old. The poet first paints the landscape in words, capturing the variety of light and shade, colours, fertile fields and barren heathlands, to suggest a satisfying harmony of disparates:

> Here waving groves a chequer'd scene display,
> And part admit, and part exclude the day ...
> There, interspersed in lawns and opening glades,
> Thin trees arise that shun each other's shades.
> Here in full light the russet plains extend:
> There, wrapt in clouds the bluish hills ascend.
> Even the wild heath displays her purple dyes,
> And 'midst the desert, fruitful fields arise,
> That crown'd with tufted trees and springing corn,
> Like verdant isles the sable waste adorn.

This is a land from which all blessings flow.

Pope then writes of the Forest's seasonal sports: shooting, hunting, fishing. He probably saw Queen Anne enjoying the chase in her high-wheeled hunting chariot and responded to the excitement, yet as an animal lover he hated the infliction of suffering on any small creature. He describes the death of a pheasant, a bird still bred for the gun, interplaying the jewel colours of the living bird and its fiery, flaming death:

> See! from the brake the whirring pheasant springs,
> And mounts exulting on triumphant wings:
> Short is his joy; he feels the fiery wound,
> Flutters in blood, and panting beats the ground,
> Ah! what avail his glossy, varying dyes,
> His purple crest, and scarlet-circled eyes,
> The vivid green his shining plumes unfold,
> His painted wings and breast that flames with gold?

Even more poignant are the lines describing the shooting of small song-birds:

> Oft, as the mounting larks their notes prepare,
> They fall, and leave their little lives in air.

A shooting scene by the engraver Thomas Bewick

Contrasted with the pastoral idyll is the turbulence of English history manifested by Windsor Castle. But both bloody civil strife and the recent "inglorious triumphs" of war are ended now in the Queen's goddess-like declaration of peace:

> At length great Anna said, "Let discord cease!"
> She said, the world obey'd, and all was peace!

Surely in these lines Pope must have in mind the statue of the Queen, placed in a niche in the Guildhall, from where she gazes loftily down on her subjects. It was inscribed "Annae vis similem sculpere? Sculpe Deam", translated as "Would'st thou shew Anna? Set a goddess to our view".

The poem concludes with a vision of Britain posting its ships in trade to the four corners of the world, with future prosperity based on its wealth of timber for ship-construction:

> Thy trees, fair Windsor! now shall leave their woods,
> And half thy forest rush into thy floods ...
> The time shall come, when free as seas or wind
> Unbounded Thames shall flow for all mankind,
> Whole nations enter with each swelling tide,
> And seas but join the regions they divide.

With Britain leading the way in establishing free trade, a harmony of man will be established, equal to the harmony of the Forest landscape.

Alas, optimism soon disappeared after Anne's death in the next year. A German duke succeeded to the throne as George I, and a Jacobite rebellion in favour of James II's Catholic son brought renewed bloodshed; Pope's father was driven from Binfield by further anti-Catholicism. To Pope and Swift it seemed that greed, graft and ignorance triumphed in public life, and they picked up their pens in attack.

Swift came back to England in 1726, staying with Pope in his riverside home at Twickenham to prepare for the publication of his most famous work, *Gulliver's Travels*. His book satirises contemporary politicians and ideas, yet such is the attraction of Gulliver's journeys to miniature Lilliput and giant Brobdingnag that Swift's work has become a classic, especially for children. How ironic! For his overall view of man, expressed in the book's later sections, is uncompromisingly harsh. But his stay at Twickenham was a happy one: it is said that the two writers revisited Windsor Forest together, to see again the landscape which had meant so much to both.

CHAPTER SIX

Men of Letters

Horace Walpole (1717-1797), [Thomas Gray (1716-71)], Samuel Johnson (1709-84)

Horace Walpole

THROUGHOUT ITS HISTORY the Castle has gone through cycles of neglect or damage and then restoration. In the mid-eighteenth century, when Horace Walpole rented a house in its precincts, it was in one of its neglected phases and had become a rather melancholy place. The royal family had not lived there for years, and, divided up into grace and favour apartments, it had been let out mainly to elderly aristocratic ladies. There they spent their last years in card parties, gossip, and coach rides to take the air. But this did not put off the twenty-nine year-old frequenter of fashionable gaming clubs, masquerades and theatres, from choosing a ''little tub of forty pounds a year'' in the summer of 1746 as a refuge from the non-stop pace of town life. To one of his many correspondents he wrote from Windsor, and broke the surprising news that he had

> got into a new scene... I am retired hither like an old summer dowager; only that I have no toad-eater [*flatterer*] to take the air with me in the back part of my lozenge coach [*coach with coat of arms*] and to be scolded.

Horace Walpole, ''Horry'' to his friends, was the youngest son of Sir Robert Walpole, the statesman who dominated politics in the first half of the century. He had died the previous year, leaving his son a house in London where he established a reputation as a dandy and a dilettante, and where as a

Member of Parliament he occasionally attended the House of Commons. Horry had been educated at Eton where he formed several friendships, one of them with Thomas Gray, the poet associated with Stoke Poges and 'The Elegy in a Country Churchyard'. Gray wrote teasingly to his friend "in his rural capacity, snug in his tub on Windsor Hill", comparing him with a pregnant society beauty who slips away into the country in order to

> be brought to bed perhaps of twins, and whisk to town again the week after with a face as if nothing had happened.

For smart young men about town Windsor was a backwater.

The snug little tub didn't suit Walpole for long and he gave it up before the end of the year, but probably not because of the old dowagers, whose tea and tittle-tattle he enjoyed life-long. He still wanted a house of his own away from London, but one with land and possibilities for development. Like most young men of means he had been on the Grand Tour and wanted to display the treasures with which he had returned, and to make the building in which they were housed an expression of his personality and cultural tastes.

Three years later Walpole bought a property called Strawberry Hill by the Thames at Twickenham, and spent the rest of his life transforming it. A small undistinguished house metamorphosed into a Gothic extravaganza, its architecture a fantasy concoction of elements from medieval castles and churches. The "toy castle" became a showpiece, crammed with curiosities, adorned with painted glass, tapestries and coats of arms. Though architecturally it was a historical jumble, creating its effects out of lath and plaster rather than stone (its "battlements" needed frequent renewal), "Strawberry Hill Gothic" came to be a recognised building style. The house aroused so much interest in Walpole's lifetime that he issued tickets to view; today as part of a training college the building still attracts many visitors.

But he wasn't the first such idiosyncratic builder: in developing Strawberry Hill Walpole was influenced by his friend Richard Bateman who, living by the Thames at Old Windsor, had some years earlier shown how it could be done. Dicky Bateman, son of an influential City man, had bought a similarly small dwelling and transformed it, except that in his case the exotic inspiration was Chinese, or as he termed it "Sharawadgi", though no-one knew exactly what that meant. His house was full of Chinoiserie, and his garden of pagodas, temples and willow-pattern bridges. But after he had seen Strawberry Hill, master turned pupil. Walpole boasted that he had "converted Dicky Bateman from a Chinese to a Goth... I preached so effectually that his every pagoda took the veil". Now Bateman's home became "a monastery": it is still known as The Priory.

Like Strawberry Hill, the house was Gothicised with pointed windows, towers and battlements, a chapel and a "cloister" for monkish contemplation. Oblivious to propriety Bateman brought from a real abbey the thirteenth-century tomb of Bishop Caducanus and set it up in the garden, claiming the Bishop as "founder" of his Priory order. Indoors there was the same profusion of stained glass and ancient nicknacks as at Strawberry Hill, though in defiance of the medieval theme Bateman kept many Chinese curios on display as well.

Walpole visited Bateman's regularly, and was jealous of some of his friend's possessions, especially a collection of old wooden chairs which had been picked up for a few shillings each from farmhouses in Herefordshire. Prizing their oddity he described them as being mainly triangular, "but all of various patterns, and carved or turned in the most uncouth and whimsical forms". He hoped to be able to pick up similar chairs himself, but was out of luck until with the death of his friend he was able to buy what he had a long time coveted.

It is interesting to think that there might have been at Old Windsor a showplace Gothic fantasy house to rival Strawberry Hill, but at Bateman's death in 1773 his heir broke up the collection and sold the lot. Walpole was

The Priory, Old Windsor

appalled, not least to think that the same fate might befall his own beloved home. He wrote to a friend:

> I went to Old Windsor to see poor Mr. Bateman's auction. It was a melancholy sight to me in more lights than one. I have spent many pleasing days there with him... and felt additional pain by reflection on my child, Strawberry. All pulled to pieces, and sold by the person he loved and left it to.

But the sale did provide opportunity for acquisition, though he wrote that it was for Bateman's sake that he had "purchased a cargo of ancient chairs, and they at least have found a resting-place in their old age". They cost Walpole just over £13 and were placed in his cloister, where they no doubt gave pleasure in his own old age.

Richard Bateman and Thomas Gray were not Walpole's only friends in the Windsor area, and he had relations too, chief among them his beautiful niece Maria, Lady Waldegrave. She likewise had a fine property, the mansion on the top of St Leonard's Hill which commanded one of the best views of the Castle. Lady Waldegrave got into trouble with the court when she took as second husband the Duke of Gloucester, King George III's brother. Her uncle had discouraged the relationship, but when Maria sent her relatives a letter of confession in 1771, Walpole wrote admiringly:

> I, a writer in some esteem, and all my life a letter-writer, never penned anything like this letter of my niece.

He now risked his own position in society and gave the couple his support, asking if he might come and kiss their hands.

As he claims, Walpole was by then an established literary figure, his most popular work being *The Castle of Otranto*, a Gothic novel which he saw as Strawberry's child and which is as extraordinary a fantasy as its parent. But his greatest claim to fame lies in his more than four thousand letters, written over sixty years to his many friends on all subjects, from the great political events of the day to the trivia of everyday life. Together they create a comprehensive picture of the eighteenth century.

Dr Samuel Johnson

Generous in friendship, Walpole was also a good hater, and one contemporary whom he did not like and vilified in his letters was the eminent Dr Samuel Johnson. The two men could not have been more different in temperament or appearance, though they did have a Windsor friend in common. Walpole, politically a Whig, was short and slight and a man who, as he could afford to do, took pride in dressing in the height of fashion.

The Tory Johnson was a great shambling giant notorious for his scruffy clothing and unkempt appearance, partly occasioned by poverty. More to be described as a man of letters than a letter-writer, he was renowned for his scholarship, his most prestigious work being his *Dictionary of the English Language*, a nine years labour.

The Windsor friend to both was Topham Beauclerk, great-grandson of Charles II and Nell Gwyn. His Christian name came from his god-father who had left him a house called Pilgrim Place near Bachelor's Acre. Beauclerk lived up to the reputations of his great-grandparents and was on the surface an unlikely friend for the moral Johnson, who was also twenty years his senior. But when Johnson first met Beauclerk at Oxford he was greatly taken with the young man's lively wit and as James Boswell, his biographer, put it "the moral, pious Johnson, and the gay, dissipated Beauclerk" became companions. Boswell says that Johnson went to stay with Beauclerk in Windsor in 1852 when in his mid-forties, and narrates an anecdote of the occasion. On a fine Sunday morning Johnson was persuaded to go out for a stroll rather than attend divine service. At one point the two men entered a church-yard while a service was in progress, yet Johnson

> laid himself down at his ease upon one of the tomb-stones. "Now, Sir (said Beauclerk) you are like Hogarth's Idle Apprentice."

Boswell gives no clue as to where to picture the scholar's great bulk adorning one of the table-top graves, but the story does show how indulged Beauclerk was as a friend, for Johnson was usually quick to put down impudence. His affection for Beauclerk endured, and when the younger man was dying in 1780 he declared in a faltering voice that he "would walk to the extent of the diameter of the earth to save Beauclerk".

His feelings were not echoed by Walpole, who professed himself quite unmoved by Beauclerk's death. Walpole had known both Beauclerk and his wife, Lady Diana, well—he had attended Richard Bateman's auction in their company—and he had a particular admiration for the former Lady Diana Spencer, known to him as Lady Di. For her paintings illustrating his tragedy *The Mysterious Mother* he created the "Beauclerk Closet" at Strawberry Hill. But Lady Di was ill-treated by her husband, and Walpole had long wished Beauclerk dead.

He was not very generous either in his comments about Johnson when he died four years later. He had liked neither Johnson's politics nor the "teeth-breaking diction" of his writings, nor his famed combativeness in conversation. What Walpole found boorish is well illustrated in another of Boswell's anecdotes, concerning a meeting in the year of Johnson's death with "a dull country magistrate" whom he identifies as the Mayor of Windsor. This man held forth at windy length about a case he'd presided over which resulted in four men being sentenced to transportation. Fidgetting to be rid of an unwelcome companion Johnson is supposed to have exclaimed "I heartily wish, sir, that I were a fifth".

Both Johnson and Walpole were revered by their contemporaries; Johnson was given the soubriquet "Dictionary", while by the end of his life Walpole, builder of Strawberry Hill and collector of curios, had become a collector's piece himself. He had become, it was said, "as much of a curiosity to all foreigners as the tombs in Westminster Abbey and the lions in the Tower".

CHAPTER SEVEN

Faithful Handmaid

Fanny Burney (1752-1840), [James Boswell (1740-95)], Dorothy Wordsworth (1771-1855)

> Melancholy—most melancholy—was the return; destitute of all that could solace, compose, or delight; replete with whatever could fatigue, harass, and depress.

Fanny Burney

It was with these gloomy words that the novelist and diarist Fanny Burney described her return in 1788 to Windsor Castle, where she had for two years been Second Keeper of the Robes to Queen Charlotte, wife of King George III.

Fanny had entered the Queen's service when she was thirty-five years old; a witty and relaxed woman with friends, she was painfully shy with strangers and had been very apprehensive about the post, but her father, the music historian Charles Burney, was delighted for the honour to come his daughter's way, and Fanny had agreed to accept it. At a time when young women were discouraged from reading let alone writing fiction, Fanny had become known for two novels of the problems of young girls in society, the lively *Evelina* and the more tearful *Cecilia*. *Evelina*, subtitled "The History of a Young Lady's Entrance into the World", was an instant success when published anonymously in 1778. As is the way of things the identity of the novelist eventually got about, and shy Fanny found herself in demand, her company sought by leading intellectuals of the day, including the founder of the Royal Academy Sir Joshua Reynolds, and Dr Johnson, of whom she became very fond.

Another of Fanny's friends was old Mrs Delany, a woman remembered now for her paper "mosaicks", exact and beautiful flower portraits made of hundreds of tiny pieces of coloured paper, precisely cut and assembled on black backgrounds. She was loved by the royal family who had provided her with a house in St Alban's Street, close to the Castle, where they frequently visited her. Mrs Delany in turn engineered a meeting between the King and Queen and Fanny, and though Fanny was almost paralysed by nerves she somehow got through the occasion. The offer of a post followed in the next year, largely to please Mrs Delany.

As Fanny had feared, it wasn't an easy life, dominated not only by her duties but also the demands of rigid court etiquette. "Directions for coughing, sneezing, or moving, before the King and Queen", sent to one of her sisters before her court appointment, comically exaggerates, but gives an idea of how formidable the rules were:

> In the first place, you must not cough. If you find a cough tickling in your throat, you must arrest it from making any sound; if you find yourself choking with the violence, you must choke—but not cough.
>
> In the second place, you must not sneeze... if the violence of the repulse breaks some blood-vessel, you must break the blood vessel—but not sneeze.
>
> In the third place, you must not, upon any account, stir either hand or foot. If, by chance, a black pin runs into your head, you must not take it out... If, however, the agony is very great, you may, privately, bite the inside of your cheek, or of your lips, for a little relief... if you even gnaw a piece out, it will not be minded, only be sure to swallow it, or commit it to a corner of the inside of your mouth till they are gone—for you must not spit.

The royal family was living at the time in Queen's Lodge, near the South Terrace of the Castle, a barrack-like building commissioned by George III to accommodate his large family (it was later demolished by George IV). Fanny was given an apartment, a servant, and a salary of £200 a year.

Her principal duty was to help the Queen to dress. Summoned by a bell to her first attendance around 7.30 a.m., Fanny would rush down the draughty corridors to the Queen's apartments to robe her in her morning wear. Each garment was in turn handed by the Wardrobe Mistress to Fanny, who thought it as well she didn't have to select the items herself for "I should run a prodigious risk of giving the gown before the hoop [*to hold out the skirt*], and

King George III, Queen Charlotte and the six princesses: a silhouette painting on glass attributed to William Rought of Oxford. © Her Majesty Queen Elizabeth II

the fan before the neck-kerchief''. Unfortunately she wasn't nimble-fingered, and being short-sighted, but forbidden by etiquette from wearing her spectacles, frequently tangled the Queen's hair with the fastenings of her necklace.

The dressing session over, ''the most pleasant part of the day'' followed when Fanny had time for breakfast, with a book for company. Then she had to put on her own court robes. A second summons came at a quarter to twelve for attendance till three o'clock, but twice a week there would also be an earlier call to help with the Queen's hairdressing. Hair styles then were extraordinarily elaborate, real and false hair drawn into high ''beehive'' shapes, curled, crimped, pinned, pommaded, powdered, beribboned and bejewelled, the process taking two to three hours to complete.

More freedom followed, a ''dear and quiet'' time, when she could write letters or keep up her diary, before dinner at five o'clock and a series of social engagements. If obliged to attend a royal function she would have to stand silent and rigid for hours. The last official call came between eleven and midnight to attend to undressing and preparing the Queen for bed. When Fanny at last got to bed herself she could hope for only a few hours sleep before the whole performance began again.

Other duties included looking after the Queen's pet dog and, a task nervously undertaken at first, preparing Her Majesty's snuff. Demanding and tedious though her daily routine was, Fanny liked and respected Queen Charlotte, and grew very fond of the six beautiful princesses, from (when she first met them) the twenty-year-old Princess Royal to the King's favourite child, the engaging three-year-old Amelia. The whole royal family responded to Fanny with warmth too, and if only the toil could have been taken from the toilette, as Fanny sighed, she might have adapted to Castle life. It had its enjoyable aspects: until her death Fanny could visit her beloved Mrs Delany almost daily, and take walks in the Park and along the Thames; she went to Egham races in their season, and accompanied the royal family on trips to London and the country. Because she trusted her, the Queen sent Fanny to attend and bring back reports from the trial of Warren Hastings, unjustly impeached for corruption while Governor-General of India (he lived at Beaumont Lodge in Old Windsor).

But there was one person in the court who made life intolerable for Fanny: Mrs Schwellenberg, the ogress who controlled most of her off-duty hours. She had come to England from Germany with Queen Charlotte at the time of her marriage to George III, and was Principal Keeper of the Robes. She was devoted to her mistress, but known amongst the courtiers for her capricious temper. Fanny nicknamed her "Cerbera", a female form of Cerberus, the dog who guarded Hades. Though Mrs Schwellenberg could be pleasant, Fanny was often made miserable by bad-tempered bullying and spiteful sneers. Possibly Fanny was over-sensitive, but nothing could have reconciled her to the tedium she had to endure every evening when expected to dine at Mrs Schwellenberg's table and afterwards engage in the card-game picquet. "O picquet!" she bursts out in her diary, "life hardly hangs on earth during its compulsion, in these months succeeding months, and years creeping, crawling, after years".

But she did get some sort of revenge in her diary, where she could ridicule Schwelly's eccentricities and imperfect command of English:

> What a stare was drawn from our new equerry... by Major Price's gravely asking Mrs Schwellenberg after the health of her Frogs! She answered that they were very well, and the Major said, 'You must know, Colonel Gwynn, Mrs Schwellenberg keeps a pair of Frogs.'
>
> 'Of Frogs?—pray what do they feed upon?'
>
> 'Flies, sir,' she answered.

Eighteenth-century view of Windsor showing the Castle and two churches

> 'And pray, ma'am, what food have they in winter?'
> 'Nothing other.'
> The stare was now still wider.
> 'But I can make them croak when I will,' she added; 'when I only go so to my snuffbox, knock, knock, knock, they croak all what I please.'

Leaguing up with the equerries against Schwelly and engaging in some mild flirtation with them, also gave Fanny relief from her oppressive companion. It was difficult for her to invite friends from her past life and the rule "no men—none", was strictly enforced. It was therefore an embarrassment when James Boswell, biographer of Dr Johnson, came to view the newly-refurbished St George's Chapel, and wanted to see Fanny too. She met him at the Chapel, delighted to see his "comic-serious face", but when he began "My dear ma'am, why do you stay?—it won't do, ma'am! you must resign!—we can put up with it no longer", she fled horrified that he might be overheard. Undaunted he pursued her, still urging her resignation—"If you do not quit, ma'am, very soon, some violent measures, I assure you, will be taken"—right to the rails of Queen's Lodge, from a window of which a disapproving and suspicious Mrs Schwellenberg gazed down.

In fact, Boswell had an ulterior motive for seeing Fanny and wanting to get her away from the Castle, and she another reason for running away: he hoped that she could help with his biography of Dr Johnson by lending "some of his beautiful billets to yourself". Fanny told him firmly that she had no letters to hand, and resisted all his suggestions for obtaining them. For once Mrs Schwellenberg was something of a refuge.

But Boswell was right that Fanny shouldn't have been cloistered as a royal handmaiden. Neither physically nor temperamentally was she fitted for such a self-sacrificing life; yet we have to be glad that she did endure five years of it, since her diary paints such a vivid picture of court life, including the first period of George III's madness, which began in October 1788 and lasted six terrible months.

Fanny movingly and dramatically records the onset of the King's disorder, the day to day anxiety as his condition fluctuated, and the terror of the Queen and the whole court as lunacy gained control (it is now thought to have been at least partly caused by physical disease). Once again it was Fanny to whom the Queen turned to bring her reports of the King, and Fanny had to exercise the utmost discretion in being neither too gloomy nor too hopeful. On one occasion she was asked to listen to what the King, in hoarse non-stop speech, was saying in the room next door:

> Nothing could be more afflicting as this task; even now it brings fresh to my ear his poor exhausted voice. 'I am nervous,' he cried; 'I am not ill, but I am nervous: if you would know what is the matter with me, I am nervous...' This was what he kept saying almost constantly, mixed in with other matter, but always returning, and in a voice that truly will never cease vibrating in my recollection.

Eventually the King's doctors recommended that he leave Windsor for Kew (the King hated Kew, but it was more secluded than Windsor), and Fanny followed with her mistress and others of the royal household for a winter in Kew's dark, cold, and even more draughty apartments. But with spring came renewed hope: Fanny was horribly alarmed while on a walk in the gardens to come face to face with the King, accompanied by his doctors. The King demanded that Fanny stop and speak to him. She turned and fled, but he pursued her calling out "Miss Burney! Miss Burney!" Finally the doctors too ordered her to stop, and she nervously engaged in conversation with the King. But while they talked she came to realise that he was almost himself again, and she was able to speed to the Queen with truly good news. On 14 March 1789 the court made a triumphant return to Windsor, and on this occasion Fanny was only too happy to be there:

> All Windsor came out to meet the King. It was a joy amounting to extacy; I could not keep my eyes dry all day long.

The town contributed forty guineas for a celebratory firework display, which the royal family watched from Mrs Schwellenberg's windows, Fanny from the room beneath.

In 1791, ten days short of five years in the Queen's service, Fanny left it. By then the strain she'd endured was under-mining her health and her gift for writing social comedy seemed to have left her. Reluctant though the Queen was to see her go (and so, curiously, was Schwelly) she bore Fanny no grudge and settled an annual pension of £100 on her. For a while this became virtually Fanny's sole support when she married General Alexandre d'Arblay, a French nobleman who'd fled penniless from the Revolution. She especially appreciated the royal family's recognition of her husband during years when, political exile or not, the French were enemies.

Fanny began to write again, and felt very honoured that Queen Charlotte allowed her to dedicate *Camilla* to her. She came to Windsor carrying ten books: one set of her five-volume work was for the Queen and another for the King, who was delighted to learn that Fanny's father had not yet received copies so he could read it first. The King received Fanny's husband on the Terrace and, it transpired many years later, the Queen peeped from her window to get a glimpse of him.

Fanny was extremely happy in her marriage, and had a son named after his father. In March 1798 the Queen invited her to bring him to see her; proud but nervous, she dressed three-year-old Alex in a new muslin frock and sash for the occasion. The princesses came in turn to see him and loaded him with toys, but Fanny was chagrined that he would not thank them with kisses. Princess Augusta (her favourite princess) was having her hair done, and Alex gazed in amazement at what was happening to her head. Only to Princess Amelia would he allow hugs and kisses: perhaps because he'd seen this youngest princess, who wouldn't stand on etiquette, kissing and being kissed by his mother. Then came the summons to Queen Charlotte. She had a Noah's Ark ready for Alex

Ark ready for Alex and he picked out the animals one by one; when any appeared which he knew he "capered with joy":

> But at the Dog, he clapped his little hands, & running close to her Majesty, leant upon her lap, exclaiming 'O! it's Bow Wow!'
>
> 'And do you know this, little Man?' said the Queen, shewing him a Cat.
>
> 'Yes,' cried he, again jumping as he leant upon her, 'its name is talled Pussy!'

Alex got restless when the Queen wanted serious conversation with his mother, and had to be quietened with a cake ("Sanky, Queen"), and altogether Fanny was "a good deal fidgetted lest he should come to some disgrace", but she reckoned that she "escaped pretty well" and they went home laden with the toys. When he grew up Alex had cause to be even more grateful to the royal family as it was through their influence that he obtained a scholarship to Cambridge. And Fanny herself, their "faithful handmaid" as she described herself, loved and kept in touch with the family to the end of her long life.

In her diary Fanny Burney often referred to the court as a "monastery". She never realised it, but for the six seemingly happy princesses court life was often a misery too: they called it the "nunnery", being kept in seclusion from eligible young men by parents who couldn't bear the thought of their marrying and leaving. One of the rituals with which Fanny was very familiar and which they loathed was "terracing", when George III paraded on the Castle Terrace with his wife and children, a spectacle which was, however, much enjoyed by the people of Windsor and their visitors. One of these in the autumn of 1792 was twenty-one year old Dorothy Wordsworth, sister of the poet William, and like Fanny a diarist and letter writer.

Dorothy Wordsworth

Dorothy came with her uncle and aunt to the Cloisters of St George's Chapel. The Reverend William Cookson, former tutor to the princes, had been made a Canon of Windsor and was taking up the obliged three months annual residence. Dorothy, orphaned at eleven and penniless, had been given a home with them and was happily helping with their four children. She found the Cloisters a friendly place to be, like one large family where "we can visit each other's houses in all Weathers without Hat or cloak". She also made friends with two young women staying in the town with their uncle, Dr William Heberden (well-known to Fanny as one of the King's physicians). Dorothy was a great walker, and she delighted that her friends were country ladies too, fond of "the Country Lady's Amusement, walking" and happy to join with her in exploring the parks, riverside and woodlands.

Dorothy's social amusements were much like Fanny's, but without the circumscriptions of royal etiquette. She too went to the Egham Races at Runnymede, taken in their coach by the Heberdens, who took her as well to St Leonard's Hill, the grand house where Horace Walpole's niece had lived. Dorothy thought it "one of the most beautiful places in Windsor" with a "noble view of Windsor Castle and of hills richly wooded".

There were also assemblies (an important part of a town's social life, when people met for conversation, card-playing and dancing, in the main public rooms: in Windsor, the Guildhall). Dorothy made her first such appearance at one of the Egham Race Balls, suffering from "the most severe tremblings and palpitations". A Young Lady making her Entrance into the World ought to have caught the eye of an eligible young gentleman, but after first suffering from a "wretched" partner she was quite happy to spend the rest of the evening dancing comfortably with one of Dr Heberden's sons, without a hint of romance.

She marvelled both at the "immense" size of the Castle, and the beauty of the Little Park just below. From the terrace she watched Queen Charlotte riding in and out of the trees in a Phaeton drawn by four white ponies. What impressed Dorothy most, however, were the evening parades of the whole royal family on the terrace. While the princesses were no doubt hating every moment, for Dorothy the occasions were magical. She wrote to a friend:

> When I first set Foot upon the Terrace I could scarcely persuade myself of the Reality of the Scene. I fancied myself treading upon Fairy-Ground, and the gay company around me was brought there by Enchantment. The King and several of the Princesses were advanc-

> ing, the Queen's band was playing most delightfully and all around me I saw only well-dressed, smart People.

Despite its being the time of the French Revolution George III strolled about with easy informality, and Dorothy joked:

> The King stopped to talk with my Uncle and Aunt, and to play with the children, who though not acquainted with the new-fangled Doctrine of Liberty and Equality, thought a King's Stick as fair Game as any other man's, and that princesses were not better than mere Cousin Dollys.

Like Fanny, Dorothy thought it "impossible to see the King and his Family at Windsor without loving them". The King's good nature showed itself particularly in his affection for children and he paid much attention to her uncle's:

> Mary he considers as a great Beauty and desired the Duke of York [*his second son*] to come from one Side of the Terrace to the other to look at her. The first time she appeared before him she had an unbecoming and rather a shabby hat on. We had then got her a new one. 'Ah' says he, 'Mary that's a pretty hat!'

Perhaps George III was wiser than his daughters knew in "terracing", mixing in this friendly way with the people only a few months before King Louis XVI of France was guillotined. Dorothy's brother William was at this same time in France enthusing over the new Republic. But time and the Revolution's excesses modified the poet's views, and in 1802 brother and sister came together for a visit to Windsor (later William was to become a pillar of the establishment, created Poet-Laureate by George III's granddaughter, Victoria). On this occasion Dorothy was pleased to note that their uncle and aunt were both well and the children— now six of them—"as good and sweet a set... as ever I was with". Both brother and sister were to return to the Windsor area in later life, by which time their uncle and family had moved to Binfield. Did they, one wonders, seek out Pope's tree and trace the inscription on it?

CHAPTER EIGHT

Citizen

Charles Knight (1791-1873), [Sir Walter Scott (1771-1832)]

THE NAME Charles Knight is not widely known nowadays. It should be: not so much for his writing, though he did write a number of books and articles, as for his pioneering work as a publisher of good cheap reading matter for the working classes. Knight was one of the great nineteenth-century crusaders; but while men like Wilberforce and Shaftesbury are remembered for the work they did in freeing men, women and children from the physical bonds of slavery or appalling working conditions, Knight, who freed their minds, is largely forgotten.

Charles Knight

He was born in Windsor in 1791 (the year Fanny Burney left the royal service) and, his mother having died when he was young, lived with his father, another Charles Knight, who kept a bookshop at 2 Castle Hill. He was a distinguished Windsor citizen himself, becoming Mayor twice, and writing what remained for half a century the standard guide to the town.

In old age Knight wrote his autobiography, *Passages of a Working Life*, long out of print, which gives a vivid picture of the Windsor of his youth. The nineteenth century was one of great change, as Knight was well aware when describing his childhood. He comments wryly, for example, on the occasion when he was taken to see the remains of highwaymen still hanging from the gibbets on Hounslow Heath—"That was a holiday sight for a schoolboy, sixty years ago!" But the most horrific revelation of his autobiography is of the insanitary conditions in the town then. An open sewer crept past the back of their house, while in Bachelor's Acre children played beside an open cesspool "kept brimming and overflowing by drains disgorging from every street". The Goswell fields below the town were "pestilent with black ditches". Neither the court nor the municipal authorities seemed to care that there was no escaping the stench, which even in the fields around Frogmore "tainted the cowslip and hawthorn blossom". No wonder that Knight contracted typhus as a child.

He was well aware of Castle life, describing the royal family as living "in a glass house" since the public had access to all parts of the Castle grounds and Park. For the children the Castle terraces provided an adventure playground, where bold boys ran fearlessly along the parapets of even the precipitous north terrace. The King was a familiar sight, "a portly gentleman with a star on his breast", whom young Charles sometimes met and bowed to in Frogmore fields. Farmer George, as mockers styled him, would be on his way to the dairy. When he grew up Knight recognised the King's political failings but, like Fanny and Dorothy, also respected the "homely kindness of his nature", and commented on his ability to recognise people. A king who knows you by name and stops for a chat is not one you can easily scorn.

Knight tells a good anecdote of George III related by his father, from 1791. Tom Paine's *Rights of Man*, a contentious political treatise sympathetic to the French Revolution, had just been published. One morning a familiar cry of "Knight, Knight" was heard in the shop. The book-seller hurried in and saw the King already sitting with a book:

> Horror! the King has taken up the dreadful *Rights of Man*... Absorbed Majesty continued reading for half an hour. The King went away without a remark; but he never afterwards expressed his displeasure, or withdrew his countenance.

George III, often ridiculed for stupidity, kept his counsel in the years of political turmoil, and also kept his throne.

Charles was sent to boarding school, but in his fourteenth year he was allowed home to watch the Garter procession. Such was the excitement and enthusiasm that on the day before the ceremony the road from London to Windsor was one long traffic jam of coaches. The boy had a seat on a Castle parapet so that he could look down on the procession as it passed to St George's Chapel from the Norman Gateway. But judged as recreation of the splendours of King Edward III and his knights, the occasion was an anticlimax:

> The old King marched erect; and the Prince of Wales bore himself proudly... but my Lord of Salisbury, and my Lord of Chesterfield,

> and my Lord of Winchilsea, and half a dozen other lords,—what a frightful spectacle of fat, limping, leaden supporters of chivalry did they exhibit to my astonished eyes!

In 1812, when Knight came of age, he joined with his father in launching a weekly newspaper, *The Windsor and Eton Express*, still going strong today. The first four-page edition was produced on 1 August. It was a brave venture in the difficult political climate of the Napoleonic Wars in which England was then engaged. Journalists had to be careful what they wrote (at this very time William Cobbett was in jail for "political libel" because he had criticised the use of flogging as an army punishment). To restrict comment newspaper tax was kept high and paper expensive, so a cheap newspaper was impossible. *The Windsor Express* cost seven old pence, which made it expensive.

Before each *Express* was printed, the Knights wanted to have the latest news from the capital. In the days before rail or telegraph, this meant that the London papers had to be sent by coach to Staines and then by a further coach service to Windsor. If the timings worked out on publication evening there would then be three-quarters of an hour to absorb and select the news, set up

2 Castle Hill, birthplace of Charles Knight

the print and produce enough copies to despatch to post-offices in Staines and Maidenhead by mail-cart. The printing process itself was laborious: until the steam press revolution it took two men an hour to handprint 250 impressions of just one side of the paper.

Knight continued as editor of the *Express* for many years, coming back to Windsor to set it up even after he had left the town. He confesses that he often found local news an "insipid dish", and that he felt constrained by working as a journalist "under the shadow of the Castle". Yet the Castle did provide good news items, as when in the year after the paper was launched the coffin of Charles I was discovered, a pointed beard still recognisable on the severed head. There were also royal funerals to write about, including that of Princess Charlotte who died in childbirth (she was the only child of the Prince Regent and as popular with the people as he was unpopular). But the funeral was a shambles: Knight had a ticket, but despite this he and others were refused entry to St George's Chapel by insolent soldiers:

> For an hour I was buffeted about, with my unfortunate companions, who comprised some of the most respectable inhabitants of Windsor; sometimes collared by the soldiers, sometimes jammed against the castle wall, and at all times insulted by dogmatical assertions or sneering indifference.

To add to the chaos the undertaker's men were "unmistakably drunk as they reeled up the steep Castle Street".

George III's funeral in 1820 was a much more decorous affair. The old king had been locked away in madness for many years, but still for Knight his death seemed the end of an era. In the following year Charles Knight senior died too, before he could see his son engaged on his most important work. Knight had always had a social conscience; he saw that the poor suffered not only physical deprivations but were also denied education and good reading material. Though there had been no revolution in England, there was much discontent, and outbreaks of mob violence. Some feared that to encourage the masses to read, thus giving them access to inflammatory political material, might make matters worse. Knight, however, believed that ignorance itself was dangerous, as well as unjust. But there was little published that was affordable for the growing number of the poor who could read, beyond the crudely sensational or the drearily religious. Novels, which Sir Walter Scott had made popular, cost one and a half guineas each (£1.57½), prohibitively dear for the less well off.

Knight planned to publish a library of good literature at a price the masses could afford, but his first attempt foundered in financial difficulties. Then he was invited to join the Society for the Diffusion of Useful Knowledge, whose members shared Knight's aims. The name sounds pompous to our ears, but "usefulness" was then a politically-acceptable criterion.

Knight was put in charge of the Society's publications. His first success was *The Penny Magazine*, launched on 31 March 1832 (as Knight notes, in the same year that the Reform Act extended the right to vote and began to shift power from the upper classes and landowners). For just one old penny a week readers could buy a four-sided magazine with well-written articles on a variety of subjects, illustrated with good quality wood-cuts. The series was so popular that in its first year two hundred thousand copies were sold, with an estimated readership of a million. One working man later wrote that he'd given up sugar in his tea to afford it.

[Just once Knight broke with normal practice and devoted a whole issue to a single subject: the death of Sir Walter Scott in 1832. Scott had himself visited Windsor some six years earlier by invitation of King George IV, who received the author with "kindness and courtesy" at the Royal Lodge. In his journal Scott records that he dined with the King and that afterwards they were entertained by the Royal Band who "lay ambushed in a green-house" nearby. The next day he was shown Windsor Castle and the contentious improvements being made by Jeffrey Wyattville, who to Scott appeared "to possess a great deal of taste and feeling for Gothic architecture". In the old apartments he noted some fine paintings and some "droll ones": these were of the King's German ancestors, "ill-coloured, orang-outang-looking figures, with black eyes and hook-noses, in old-fashion'd uniforms".]

In 1833 Knight launched *The Penny Cyclopedia*, its weekly parts building to an eight-volume work, a formula which modern publishers also use, though none has done so on such a grand scale: it took eleven years to complete, despite increasing the number of issues. Unfortunately the price had to be increased as well, with a resulting drop in sales which hit Knight hard. It was nevertheless a noble undertaking. Other ventures included a series for children, the *Library for the Young*, and various pictorial volumes; the *Pictorial Shakespeare* was the project which Knight said had given him the greatest satisfaction, distracting him from the worries of the *Cyclopedia*. In the 1840s he was able to introduce coloured plates to make the publications even more attractive.

Knight established a wide circle of friends and acquaintances from amongst Victorian society, including Charles Dickens, who took over from Scott as the most popular writer of the day. He was happily married and lived in a variety of homes in and around London. Although he never came back to live in Windsor, his autobiography shows the strong hold which his native town had on his affections and it was fitting that after his death in Addlestone in 1873 his body should have been brought back for burial in Bachelor's Acre, that dangerous playground of his youth.

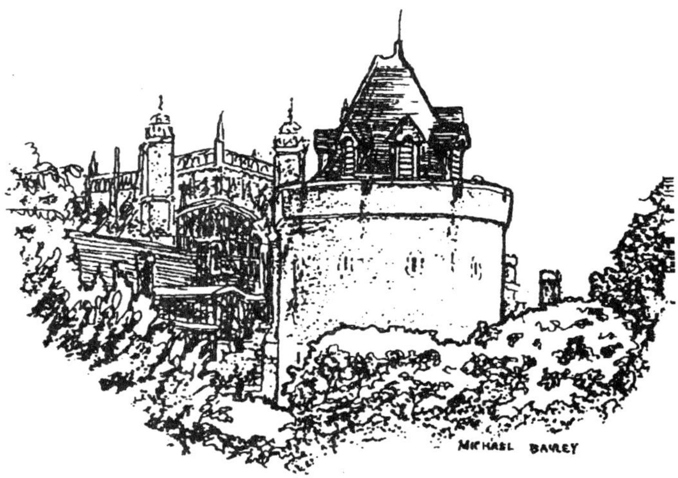

The Curfew Tower, given its present shape in 1863

CHAPTER NINE

Friends and Lovers

Percy Bysshe Shelley (1792-1822), Mary Shelley (1797-1851), Thomas Love Peacock (1785-1866)

TOWERING MOUNTAIN CRAGS and precipices, cascades tumbling from the heights into deep gorges, tumultuous torrents and mighty forests: these are the sorts of dramatic landscapes which fed the imaginations of Romantic poets such as Percy Bysshe Shelley in the early nineteenth century. Yet it was the gentler contours of Windsor Forest and the Thames Valley which, not in the mind but in reality, he cherished most dearly. To this countryside he returned again and again in his short life, bringing with him the complexities of his tangled love affairs.

Percy Bysshe Shelley

Shelley's enthusiasm for the district was fanned by his friend and fellow author Thomas Love Peacock, whom he met in 1812 as the author of a (not very good) poem, 'The Genius of the Thames'. Peacock had grown up in the area, in Chertsey and at school in Englefield Green. In some ways the friendship was of opposites, for Peacock was a rationalist and a wit with his feet firmly on the ground, whereas Shelley was impassioned and quixotic with his head in the clouds. Peacock was to make fun of some of Shelley's fads and freaks in his satirical novel *Nightmare Abbey* (1818), but his mockery was affectionate rather than scornful, for he admired his friend's brilliant imagination, enjoyed debate with him, and shared his radical political outlook. For Shelley, Peacock was a stabilising influence, and something like an older brother.

But Shelley first got to know the Windsor area long before he met Peacock, when he came as the twelve-year-old son of a baronet to Eton College. At first he was very unhappy: boys have always been quick to victimise the sensitive, the eccentric or the non-conformist, and Shelley was all three. He refused to fag, and for his moodiness and air of superiority was known as "mad Shelley" and, as one contemporary remembered, "baited like a maddened bull" till he reached "a paroxysm of anger which made his eyes flash like a tiger's, his cheeks grow pale as death, his limbs quiver, and his hair stand on end".

But with his intelligence and enthusiasms, and possessing the gift of story-telling, he was not totally friendless; another schoolfellow recalled that

> We used to wander for hours about Clewer, Frogmore, the park at Windsor, the Terrace [*of the Castle*]; and I was a delighted and willing listener to his marvellous stories of fairyland, and apparitions, and spirits and haunted ground.

All his life Shelley was interested in ghosts and the occult; once he crept from his Dame's house at midnight carrying a skull and hoping to raise a ghost, but returned terrified when, hearing rustles in the grass, he became convinced that the devil was following him.

In his later years at Eton Shelley was befriended by a distinguished Windsorian, Dr James Lind, a physician to George III and a part-time teacher at the College. Lind, tall and silver-haired, a Fellow of the Royal Society, had travelled as far afield as Iceland, India and China. He was a kindly, scholarly man, but also eccentric, and like Shelley rumoured to be interested in demonology: Fanny Burney reported fear of him as a doctor, for "his taste for tricks, conundrums, and queer things, makes people fearful of his trying experiments on their constitutions". But Shelley often took tea in his curio-crammed home in Windsor (no-one knows now where it was). Under Lind's influence he began to study systematically and he was introduced to contemporary authors like the radical William Godwin, whose *Political Justice* exerted a powerful influence. No wonder that Shelley later declared that he owed to Lind "far ah! far more than I owe to my father".

Little more than a year after leaving Eton in 1810 he had quarrelled irrevocably with his father after expulsion from Oxford for atheism; he had also eloped with and married a beautiful sixteen-year-old schoolgirl, Harriet Westbrook. For a couple of years the pair led a nomadic existence, with Shelley writing revolutionary pamphlets and, at this time of the Napoleonic Wars, alarming the authorities with his subversive opinions (though his methods of spreading them, including throwing leaflets in bottles into the

Bristol Channel, scarcely suggest that he was a very great danger to the government). It was during this time of wandering that Shelley and Peacock met, with Peacock taking a great liking to Harriet.

For a while Peacock travelled with the pair; he records how after the birth of their daughter Ianthe tension arose between them. On 19 December 1813 Shelley took a furnished house in Windsor (whereabouts unknown), but in the following April Harriet took herself away and the house was given up, apparently not without regret on Shelley's part since in a poem written then he laments his "sad and silent home" with its "desolated hearth".

Then in June Shelley met Mary Wollstonecraft Godwin, another attractive sixteen-year-old, who unlike Harriet was also intellectual. Moreover, as the daughter of the admired philosopher William Godwin and his first wife the feminist Mary Wollstonecraft, she seemed destined to be Shelley's partner. In July Shelley embarked on a second elopement, this time across the Channel. He had always been an advocate of free love and he wrote to Harriet, pregnant with his second child, expecting her to understand the situation and telling her that he would remain her "affectionate friend" for ever. He even suggested that she might like to join them in Switzerland.

On their return to London the lovers led a difficult life, with accumulating money problems, but in April 1814 they enjoyed a brief holiday at the Windmill Inn, Salt Hill, near Slough (the hill gets its name from an Eton ceremony which Shelley would have taken part in as a boy). Today the area has become totally urban, but in those days the hill was set in attractive wooded countryside and represented an escape to "green fields and acorns".

Salt Hill

Then in the summer their finances were sorted out and they dreamed of retreat from the city to a house in Windsor Forest. For help Shelley turned to Peacock, who was living in Marlow.

Peacock's sympathies in Shelley's marital affairs had been with Harriet, but he accepted the poet's friendship on his terms and helped him to find a furnished cottage, with verandah and trellised porch, at Bishopsgate just on the edge of Windsor Great Park (now known as "Shelley's House"). Apart from "odious curtains" it was perfect; in August Shelley and Mary took possession and spent the late summer days exploring the Forest. Peacock often walked the fifteen miles from Marlow to join them.

[Shelley's stay took place just a year after a major change had come to the Forest, for on 1 July 1814 Parliament had passed an Act of Enclosure for it. Peacock records a further consequence when on a clear calm sunny day he watched the deer being rounded up by the cavalry and driven within the parkland pales. He called his reminiscence 'The Last Day of Windsor Forest', for though it was, he says, the "most beautiful sight I ever witnessed", he lamented that "with the expulsion of the deer, the life of the old scenes was gone".]

Forest scene from Ainsworth's Windsor Castle

Apart from walking in the Forest Shelley loved to make himself an "open-air study" in a grove of the great old Park trees, and on fine days would sit surrounded by his books, paper leaves flapping beside him and green leaves rustling overhead. He also took a boy's delight in water, and Peacock describes how, whether he came to Virginia Water or just a small pond, he was

Shelley's House at Bishopsgate: William Shelley was born in the room above the front door.

liable to empty his pockets of letters (and bills) and create a flotilla of little boats to sail on them.

Yet he was not completely content, a conviction having seized him that he was consumptive and hadn't long to live. From his "study" he wrote gloomily to a friend:

> It is already the end of August. Those leaves have lost their summer glossiness which, when I see you again, will be fluttering in the wind of autumn. Such is mortal life.

But his health improved after a boat-trip up the Thames which he, Peacock, Mary and her brother took in September. One of the reasons for Shelley's poor health was, in Peacock's opinion, his vegetarian diet of bread and butter with tea or powdered lemonade to drink: for the boat-trip he recommended Shelley to give it up in favour of "three mutton chops, well peppered" every day.

From nearby Old Windsor they embarked in a wherry, and in perfect weather set off to find the river's source. Sleeping out under the stars on the river bank, the party rowed in a leisurely way up river beyond Lechlade until they reached a place where the boat foundered in weed, cattle blocked the way in water only inches deep, and they could go no further. By the time they reached Old Windsor again Shelley was fit and well thanks, Peacock thought, to the mutton chops.

Refreshed and invigorated he began work on his poem *Alastor*, using his open-air "study" as often as he could. The Greek title word was suggested by Peacock, for it means "the spirit of solitude", and it is a poem examining the nature of an inward-looking poet who shuns human society. Shelley used his recent expedition on the river as an image for psychological development as the "poet" journeys by boat through wild forest and mountain landscapes. The scenery of the poem is not natural but transformed to Romantic grandeur, yet in some lines, as when he writes "the woven leaves\Make network of the dark blue light of day", it is possible to sense Shelley's response to what he saw around him at Bishopsgate.

For Mary this period in their lives was probably the calmest she was ever to know with Shelley. He was well and writing, and she waiting the birth of her second baby: William Shelley was born in January of 1816.

Few visitors disturbed the peace apart from one or two close friends such as Peacock. He says that Shelley did become friendly with one local man, Dr Pope, a Quaker from Staines whom he first called in as a physician. The old man liked to discuss theology with Shelley, though the poet had at first hesitated to express his atheist views till the Quaker declared: "I like to hear thee talk, friend Shelley, I see thou art very deep".

Other callers were less welcome: one day on Egham Hill Shelley spotted someone he didn't like ahead, jumped through a hedge, ran across a field and hid in a ditch, telling startled farm-workers that he was escaping from a bailiff.

But in the summer Shelley grew restive. The house at Bishopsgate was given up and they set off for the Continent again. Even from their arrival, however, Shelley's thoughts were turning back to England and he wrote to Peacock:

> I wish you to look out for a home for me and Mary and William and the kitten, who is now en pension. I wish you to get an unfurnished house, with as good a garden as may be, near Windsor Forest.

It was to be their "fixed, settled, eternal home".

Mary Shelley

Despite the preference for the Forest, they eventually moved into Albion House in Marlow in February 1817, where their daughter Clara was born. There Mary also had the satisfaction of completing her science-fiction story *Frankenstein*, begun by the shores of Lake Geneva. It is a remarkable book for a nineteen-year-old to have conceived, and it achieved a popular success which it has never lost: the idea of a grotesque assemblage of human parts brought to life by a mad scientist has entered popular mythology, and millions who do not recognise the name Shelley know of Frankenstein's monster. But how many who have read the book remember that Mary brings the Swiss scientist Frankenstein to England and to Windsor? His intention is to to seek knowledge and find an isolated spot to create a mate for his monster, but first he embarks on a sightseeing tour with a friend. They arrive on "27th March"—an extraordinarily specific date in a novel where the years are rendered as 17--, so it must have had significance for her (could it have been the day on which she was writing?). They spend a few days at Windsor, "rambling in its beautiful forest", where the "majestic oaks, the quantity of game, and the herds of stately deer" were something for men of the mountains to marvel at.

Shelley himself wrote his long poem *The Revolt of Islam*, much of it in Bisham Woods, and there were more boating trips and very long walks, sometimes to Windsor Castle or Virginia Water and the old forest haunts. But happiness was elusive now, especially for Mary: she had become Shelley's wife, but a dark shadow always in the corner of her mind was the knowledge that the marriage had followed Harriet Shelley's suicide. From Marlow Shelley fought unsuccessfully for the custody of his children by Harriet, and it was partly out of fear that even Mary's children might be taken from them that they left the "fixed, settled, eternal" home for a wandering existence in Italy. There, by bitter irony, both William and Clara died.

From the continent Shelley wrote long, magical descriptions of scenery to Peacock. But Peacock could not be tempted to join his friend for he felt himself "rooted like a tree on the banks of one bright river". Shelley too continued to be haunted in mind by the landscapes of home: in the midst of the Apennine mountains he wrote to Peacock:

> I have seen nothing so beautiful as Virginia Water in its kind. And my thoughts forever cling to Windsor Forest, and the copses of Marlow, like the clouds which hang upon the woods of the mountains, low and trailing, and though they pass away, leave their best view when they themselves have faded.

But he never saw any of these places again. After four years of a wandering, turbulent life in Italy, during which many of his best-known poems such as the 'Ode to the West Wind' were written, he was drowned in the Gulf of Spezia. It was Peacock to whom the near-destitute Mary turned, asking him to inform Shelley's father of the tragedy (but even death couldn't reconcile the old man to his son's memory).

Feeling very much alone Mary returned to England with her remaining child Percy. She began to write again and in 1826 a new science-fiction novel, *The Last Man,* a mirror to her feelings, was published, showing her yearning after the happiness of the Windsor Forest days. The book is set towards the end of the twenty-first century (but with little attempt to suggest technological advances). England has become a republic, though Adrian, son of the last king and known as the Earl of Windsor, still lives in Windsor Castle. This Adrian, descendant presumably of the Hanoverian Kings so despised by Shelley, is, startling though it may seem, modelled on Shelley himself. To the narrator's sister Perdita he makes a gift of a little "low-roofed" cottage in Englefield Green, bordering the Forest—clearly the cottage where Mary had been so content. The characters move happily between Castle and Cottage, reading, talking, "pass[ing] whole days under the leafy covert of the forest with our books and music".

But the idyllic life is doomed: the plot turns on a horrendous plague which gradually destroys the entire human race, leaving the narrator companionless as "the last man"—just as Mary had declared she herself felt, "the last relic of a beloved race, my companions extinct before me".

CHAPTER TEN

Eminent Victorians

Charles Dickens (1812-70), Alfred Lord Tennyson (1809-83)

Charles Dickens in youth

ON 10 FEBRUARY 1840 the young Queen Victoria married Prince Albert of Saxe-Coburg in London and set off for a short honeymoon at Windsor Castle. The nation rejoiced, with a few exceptions. One of those was Charles Dickens, already well-known for his novels *The Pickwick Papers*, *Oliver Twist* and *Nicholas Nickleby*. A high-spirited and convivial young man of twenty-eight, something of a dandy with his velvet waistcoats, embroidered shirts and fancy cravats, he enjoyed being a man-about-town in the company of his bachelor friends: despite being married and already the father of three children.

Perhaps yearning to recover a bit of unencumbered romance he affected a deep passion for the royal bride and anguish at her marriage, drawing his friends John Forster and the artist Daniel Maclise into a game which was mainly fun, but just a little in earnest. (Maclise had been invited to paint the Queen's portrait as a secret present for Albert and so, lucky fellow, got to meet the goddess.) The three of them set off for Windsor on the day after the wedding in order to lament.

The wedding was a great occasion for Windsor. For the well-to-do there were public dinners and a ball at the Town Hall, while a collection was raised for the poor which provided over five thousand deprived people in Windsor and Clewer with bread, meat, and beer on the wedding day. This is an amazing figure: bearing in mind that in the 1841 census the combined populations were approximately eleven and a half thousand it means that almost half the inhabitants were living in poverty, most in the squalid slums of the Goswells area. It needed a Dickens to describe the scene, but the *Windsor Express* did its best:

> It was pleasing to see in the forenoon the numerous poor persons trudging with cheerful countenances, with good-sized pieces of beef to the bakers' shops to be cooked—to many of them a luxury which their own circumstances too often denied them.

(In those days it was customary to take joints of meat to the baker's for cooking.) In the afternoon the Teetotal Society joined in the fun and boiled kettles for a "tea and turnout" for two hundred, including thirty "reformed drunkards". Even the prisoners in the gaol got extra rations.

Victoria and Albert dancing the waltz

When daylight faded Windsor lighted up with coloured lamps (some gaslit), creating crowns, V and A initials, stars and other favours. In Eton two triumphal arches had been built. Into the fairy-tale scene came the coach carrying the Queen and her husband, the little bride dressed in white satin trimmed with swansdown, with a matching white satin bonnet. The crowds lining the route, swollen in number by hundreds of visitors, cheered loudly, and locals leaned from their windows to wave white handkerchiefs. The excitement and merry-making lasted long into the night.

Next morning many had hangovers, though Victoria and Albert were up bright and early (prompting Charles Greville's remark that "this was not the way to provide us with a Prince of Wales"). Just as the crowds were leaving Dickens and his friends arrived. To another friend he afterwards wrote in mock desperation that the three of them had:

> sallied down to Windsor, prowled about the Castle, saw the Corridor and their private rooms—nay, the very bedchamber (which we know from having been there twice) lighted up with such a ruddy, homely, brilliant glow—bespeaking so much bliss and happiness that I, your

> humble servant, lay down in the mud at the top of the long walk and refused all comfort—to the immeasurable astonishment of a few straggling passengers who had survived the drunkenness of the previous night.

Did Dickens really reach the royal bedchamber, or is he just fantasising ?

Next day he carried on the joke in a letter to Forster which mimics Burns' 'My heart's in the Highlands, my heart is not here/My heart's in the Highlands a-chasing the deer':

> I am utterly lost in misery, and can do nothing. I have been reading *Oliver*, *Pickwick*, and *Nickleby* to get my thoughts together for the new effort, but all in vain:
>
> My heart is at Windsor,
> My heart isn't here;
> My heart is at Windsor,
> A following my dear.

He claims to be suicidal, with "thoughts of the Serpentine, of the regent's canal, of the razors upstairs, of the chemist's down the street". And in mock despair he wrote (to yet another friend) of making his will, adding a last request:

> ... to be embalmed, and to be kept (if practicable) on the top of the Triumphal Arch at Buckingham Palace when she is in town, and on the north-east turrets of the Round Tower when she is at Windsor.

As other unrequited lovers he declared that "she will be sorry when I am gone". Probably Victoria would have felt a pang if the novelist had died young: she had read *Oliver Twist* the year before and found it "excessively interesting". When they eventually met in 1870, not long before Dickens' actual death, she asked him for a complete set of his works. By that time he had written a great deal, and his later novels, including *Little Dorrit*, *Great Expectations* and *Our Mutual Friend*, were much weightier books than the light-hearted earlier publications, though still with the liveliness, wealth of characterisation, and social probing which had established his reputation. Victoria was no mean writer herself, pouring out her thoughts and feelings in her diary and her huge correspondence; she also published an account of holidays at Balmoral with beloved Albert, *Journal of our Life in the Highlands* (1867), which was a popular success. Victoria later gave Dickens an autographed copy of her work in return for a shelf-ful of his.

Back in 1841, in November of the year following the wedding, Windsor became a refuge rather than a place of misery. Dickens was due to sail for America, an undertaking which involved much worry and difficult decisions about his family, now increased by a fourth child. Then came an illness, so leaving wife and family behind he set off for Windsor to recuperate at the White Hart Hotel. Very soon he was able to report that

> I am getting stout and hearty, and can walk about the Parks here like a giant with his seven-leaguers on, and eat like the same with his knife and fork in hand, and sleep like the same with a hogshead of old crusted under his waistcoat.

A decade later when his eldest son Charley went to Eton, the fees paid by the wealthy banker Angela Burdett Coutts, Dickens relished the chance for summer excursions on the river. Though he called it ''gipseying'' these were not spur-of-the-minute occasions, but meticulously planned, with parties of friends and champagne hampers ordered from Fortnum and Masons. The boatman was certainly impressed, declaring he would go no more ''with gingerbeer company'', but Dickens worried that Charley and his friends would get drunk:

Romney Lock in the 1840s

> They were very good, however. The speech of one became thick, and his eyes too like the lobster's to be comfortable, but only temporarily.

They returned in a thunderstorm which drenched them and was for the boys, Dickens said, the great success of the day.

There was one big difference between these expeditions and his first. In 1840, wearing their marriage medals next to their hearts, the three thwarted lovers left Windsor in a post chaise. Ten years later the journey from London to Eton was by train. In fact for Eton there was choice of station: Slough on the Great Western Railway from Paddington, its branch station Windsor Central (creating this line had the benefit of demolishing some of the worst slums), or Riverside Station for the connection with Waterloo on the London and South-Western line. With a change Victoria Station could also be reached. In the 1860s Dickens was to use this variety to his advantage.

By the late 1850s Dickens' marriage had turned sour. Catherine Dickens had given birth to ten children, nine of whom survived infancy; not surprisingly she had lost her figure, and wrapped up in pregnancies and ill-health she was not much of a companion either. Though he loved his children dearly, Dickens had resented the births of the later arrivals and had been inclined to see Catherine's fertility as a problem with which he was unconnected. Poor Catherine was humiliated in a separation publically attributed to "incompatibility"; no-one was to know that privately her husband had fallen in love with an actress.

Ellen Ternan (Nelly) was born in 1839, the same year as Dickens' daughter Katey. Her parents were both in the theatre and Nelly and her two older sisters were put on the stage at an early age. Mr Ternan died when Nelly was seven; the mother and three girls struggled for a living and Mrs Ternan, who specialised in Shakespearean roles, was lucky to get engagements with the leading actor of the time, William Charles Macready. (His company, including Mrs Ternan, continued after his retirement and in 1854 gave a command performance in Windsor Castle).

It was through Dickens' own love of acting that he met Nelly. In 1857 he put on an amateur production of Wilkie Collins' melodrama *The Frozen Deep*, with an accompanying farce. Queen Victoria herself went to see it, though Dickens had refused to take the production to the Palace and also declined to meet her during the performance, on the grounds that he could not present himself in a "costume and appearance that were not my own". The production went on to Manchester, but Dickens worried that it wouldn't be quite "proper" for his two daughters to take part. Professional actresses were engaged instead: Maria and Ellen Ternan. In the farce Nelly took over Katey's part as a young girl with whom an old man, played by Dickens, falls in love. Life was set to imitate art.

Dickens kept the slowly developing affair very quiet: it wouldn't have done for the great proponent of family values to be found flouting them himself. So well did the two cover their tracks that it was only in the 1930s that the truth began to emerge, and despite intense probing there are still gaps in the story of their years together.

One period of the relationship was, however, brilliantly revealed in a piece of literary detection by Felix Aylmer, published in 1959. Dickens kept diaries in which he cryptically recorded his many engagements and journeys. These he destroyed at the end of the year, with one exception, the diary for 1867 which he lost in New York. He worried a little over its loss at the time: how much more so if he had known that it would surface and be deciphered in the next century.

Aylmer noticed that whereas towns that Dickens visited by train for his solo readings from his books were written in full, certain recurring journeys were indicated only by initials. He appeared to be going to a place identified as Sl, with the initials P, W, V and D indicating points of either departure or arrival. The initial N also occurred frequently, undoubtedly for Nelly. Aylmer reasoned that Sl must stand for Slough, with W either Waterloo or Windsor, and the other initials representing Paddington, Victoria and Datchet. He then studied the ratebooks for Slough and discovered a house in the High Street, Elizabeth Cottage, where from early 1866 the rates were being paid by a man usually calling himself Charles Tringham, but sometimes John Tringham, Charles Turnan, or other variations (Tringham was the surname of the proprietor of a tobacco shop which Dickens patronised).

Strange though it may seem to us today, Dickens had chosen Slough High Street as his secret hideaway. Slough was not then the bustling town it is now but retained a village character, and it was a brilliant choice, simply because of the railway connections. Dickens' London office was just over the river from Waterloo, but Aylmer deduced that he avoided making too much use of the same route: he could travel down from Paddington to Slough in an evening and be lost in the darkness, but go back in the morning by taking the pleasant walk over the fields to either Windsor or Datchet stations, and consequently never be seen at one place too frequently.

Thus Dickens avoided attention; but he was a public figure, and was certainly recognised by some in Slough. Aylmer unearthed a *Windsor Express* of 1889 in which, following a fire in the High Street which destroyed Elizabeth Cottage along with several shops, it is stated without comment that Charles Dickens had lodged there at one time.

The older Dickens

There is a mystery in the diary: against 13 April, when Dickens is "At Sl." there is the unusual word "Arrival". A week later the word "[Loss]" occurs. At the foot of the page Dickens writes "N. ill latter part of this month". Though there's no proof, it has been speculated that this refers to the birth and death of a child. (Almost certainly a child which died young was born to the couple while Nelly was secreted in France a few years earlier.)

Whether Nelly suffered the distress of losing a baby or not, she may well have disliked being tucked away in a semi-rural backwater. A Slough girl, Jane Wheeler, was engaged as a maid; she became fond of Nelly and stayed with her for fifty years. She also had a little dog for company, grandly named Lady Clara Vere de Vere after one of Tennyson's heroines. But she wouldn't have had much to do. She may have welcomed a move from Slough to Peckham, which the diary shows was being planned before the mysterious April entries. Again as Charles Tringham, Dickens took out a lease on a new and grander property than Elizabeth Cottage: it was named Windsor Lodge.

Three years later, worn out by frantic scurryings between Peckham, Gads Hill (his official family home in Kent), and the venues of his exhausting public readings, Dickens died. All England mourned the loss of the great entertainer, social reformer and moralist, and he was buried in Westminster Abbey.

In his last year Dickens had finally come face to face with the earlier object of his admiration, Queen Victoria. In their interview both were at first reserved, but the conversation warmed up and, in Dickens' words to a friend, "it would be difficult to say what we did *not* talk about". News of his death was telegraphed to the Queen at Balmoral, and she paid him tribute in her *Journal*:

> He is a very great loss. He had a large, loving mind and the strongest sympathy with the poorer classes. He felt sure that a better feeling, a much greater union of classes would take place in time. And I pray earnestly that it may.

She commemorated the public man, knowing nothing of either his long-ago adoration of her, or the furtive private life of the "large, loving mind".

As for Nelly, now aged thirty-one but blessed with a youthful appearance, she was free to begin life again: six years later she married. Transformed into Mrs George Wharton Robinson, she became a thoroughly respectable Victorian matron with two children. Her husband might be twelve years her junior, but since she soon knocked at least ten years off her age this was of no account to society. The days of Elizabeth Cottage were firmly put behind her.

When Alfred Tennyson, the Poet Laureate, saw Millais' drawing of the dead Dickens he felt that he was looking at his own death image. Three years older than the novelist, Tennyson did bear a physical likeness to Dickens, and was aware how they were linked together as the two literary lions of the age. Both had then the kind of star status that the twentieth century has given to film, pop and sports celebrities. People queued overnight for tickets to Dickens' readings and police had sometimes to control the crowds, whilst tourists on the Isle of Wight where Tennyson lived, entered his garden and even peered through his windows to catch sight of the great man. Advertisers drew heavily and without permission on their names and writings. The two men knew and liked each other, and Tennyson was godfather to one of Dickens' sons, the grandly-named Alfred D'Orsay Tennyson Dickens.

They differed in their association with Queen Victoria however. It is obvious that after, and perhaps because of, his youthful infatuation Dickens shunned encounters with the Queen, but Tennyson as Laureate developed a warm relationship, which brought him eventually to Windsor.

Initially it was Albert who was Tennyson's admirer, and who in 1850 recommended that he succeed Wordsworth as Poet Laureate. The Prince Consort visited him at his home, and asked for an autographed copy of the *Idylls of the King*, narrative poems which rework the Arthur legend, for the Royal Library in Windsor. Following the trauma of the Prince's death in 1860

Alfred Tennyson

Princess Alice, Victoria and Albert's second daughter, suggested that Tennyson write something in her father's memory. At first agitated by the idea, he nevertheless set about composing a dedicatory poem to a new edition of the *Idylls*. Its homage to "Albert the Good" who wore "the white flower of a blameless life", and its prayer for his sorrowing widow, could not fail to please, and the Princess was instructed by the Queen to tell Tennyson how his words "soothed her aching, bleeding heart".

She turned for further comfort to *In Memoriam*, the collection of poems Tennyson published in 1850 in memory of his friend Arthur Hallam. The poet learnt that in her much read copy she had altered certain verses, for example:

> Tears of the widower, when he sees
>   A late-lost form that sleep reveals,
> And moves his doubtful arms, and feels
>   Her place is empty, fall like these...

became "Tears of the *widow*, when *she* sees..." and so on.

From this time onwards, through correspondence and occasional meetings, the Queen and Tennyson developed a special relationship. Though they are not the poems of Tennyson's which we now admire, he regularly produced verses to celebrate royal weddings and funerals. In 1864, for example, he was asked to supply lines to be engraved round the pedestal of the statue of Victoria's mother, the Duchess of Kent, which was to be placed in her Mausoleum at Frogmore. Tennyson produced:

> Long as the heart beats life within the breast
>   Thy child will bless thee, guardian-mother mild,
> And far away thy memory will be bless'd
>   By children of the children of thy child.

The Queen particularly liked "guardian-mother mild".

Frogmore Mausoleum

In 1873 Victoria asked her Poet Laureate to visit with her the "dear Mausoleum" which she had had built for Albert at Frogmore, and where she too planned to be interred. Though he wrote to his wife "How I longed to shirk it", Tennyson knew that he could not refuse the invitation. So in her *Journal* for 6 March Victoria records driving from the Castle down to the Mausoleum with Princess Beatrice and meeting the poet. He very properly admired the "dear beautiful statue" and the building, which he told her

> was very beautiful & worthy of what it was intended for. I observed that it was light and bright, which he thought a great point & went on to say that he wished funerals could be in white! Why should death, which was already so dreadful in itself, be clothed with everything to make it worse, as if it were the end of all things?

When Tennyson himself died in 1892 (by then he had accepted a peerage and become Lord Tennyson), the Queen noted with admiration that:

> He died with his hand on his Shakespeare, and the moon shining into the window, and over him. A worthy end to such a remarkable man.

She also noticed that his funeral followed that expression of his feelings to her, with his coffin covered by a white pall. So it was that Tennyson's influence left a final mark at Windsor during the Queen's own funeral, which she had planned in detail. On 1 February 1901, in bitter weather, her coffin with white and golden pall was drawn on a gun carriage through the Windsor streets to the Albert Memorial Chapel. It was almost exactly sixty-one years since she had arrived as a bride in white swansdown: were there any in the watching crowds who as children had joined in the excitement of that far-off event? Four days later, with huge crowds lining the Long Walk, the coffin was born to the final ''light, bright'' resting place at Frogmore. Appropriately the anthem at the service was a setting of words written by Tennyson (for Victoria's grandson, Albert Victor), expressing the faith which had comforted both Queen and Laureate:

> The face of Death is toward the Sun of Life,
> His shadow darkens earth: his truer name
> Is ''Onward'', no discordance in the roll
> And march of the Eternal Harmony
> Whereto the worlds beat time, tho' faintly heard
> Until the great Hereafter. Mourn in Hope !

That night a heavy fall of snow added a last touch of white. Windsor woke to find the purple drapes with which the streets had been hung brought into relief by its crisp whiteness, while in the words of the *Windsor Express,* ''The same wintry coating outlined the stately Castle battlements, frosted the trees, and covered the green lawns with a wintry mantle''. Tennyson himself would surely not have found fanciful the idea that Nature had found a way to bid farewell to the old Queen.

Footnote: *Recently I was told by Mrs Hazel Finlayson of the Runnymede Arts Association, that her father, Percy Brown, attended Queen Victoria's funeral in Windsor. He vividly remembered the awful spontaneous groan which arose from the crowd as the coffin went past.*

CHAPTER ELEVEN

Word Spinner

Margaret Oliphant (1828-97), [George Eliot (1819-80)]

> I have worked a hole in my right forefinger—with the pen, I suppose! and can't get it to heal,—also from excessive use of that little implement.

This is what the popular Victorian novelist Margaret Oliphant wrote to a friend in the year before she died. It is not surprising that she had worn a hole in her finger for there can have been few writers as productive as she: ninety-eight novels, eight volumes of short stories, twenty-five books of non-fiction, and numerous reviews and journalistic articles poured from her pen in a continuous stream. Much of this creative flood was produced in the two homes which she occupied during the thirty years that she lived in Windsor.

Margaret Oliphant

Popular though she was in her own day, with such a huge output the quality of her work was uneven, and she suffered an eclipse after her death. But recently her worth as a highly intelligent, amusing and perceptive writer has been recognised and a number of her best stories reprinted. They offer the reader great variety, from the fine social comedy *Miss Marjoribanks* where the sharply pointed satire is worthy of Jane Austen, to the dramatic *Kirsteen* set in her native Scotland, or her supernatural "tales of the seen and the unseen" which she could write only "when they come to me".

Mrs Oliphant (she was always known as such and would surely have a sharp word for anyone calling her "Margaret" or "Oliphant") was writing *Miss Marjoribanks*, when in her mid-thirties she came to Windsor looking for a home. She liked the town at once for "the beauty of the river and the castle and the air of cheerful life about". Her need of cheerfulness was then great following a series of cruel blows in her married life. First she lost two little babies. Then her artist husband Frank Oliphant (some of whose stained glass can be seen in St Mary's Church in Aylesbury) contracted tuberculosis. He died in Rome while seeking better health in a warm climate, and leaving his young wife with two small children, Maggie and Cyril, another expected and £1000 worth of debts.

Six weeks after her husband's death a second son was born (christened Francis but always known as Cecco). Only her pen stood between the family and destitution. Yet somehow Mrs Oliphant managed to pay off the debts and build a new life. Then four years later tragedy struck once more: while staying again in the fatal city of Rome her eleven-year-old Maggie caught a fever, died, and was buried beside her father.

This time it took Mrs Oliphant much longer to pick up the pieces, and she spent eighteen forlorn months wandering round the continent. But in 1865, when Cyril was nine and Cecco six, she returned to England for the sake of their education. At this time she was winning a high reputation for her writing, particularly with the series of novels, of which *Miss Marjoribanks* is one, set in a small town called Carlingford. Ambitious for her sons, she felt that she could afford to give them the best education and determined on either Eton or Harrow. Her first visit to Windsor decided her in Eton's favour and Cyril was entered for the College, with permission to live at home. So Mrs Oliphant went house-hunting.

She found just what she wanted in one of the best streets in Windsor, Clarence Crescent, created in 1820 as Windsor expanded, and named after the Duke of Clarence (afterwards William IV). Mrs Oliphant took possession of number 6, one of a pair of stuccoed house with elegant wrought iron balconies, a "very bright" house on which the sun shone almost all day long. It had a little garden behind and, more importantly, the communal Crescent garden in front. The family called it "the Plantation" and they had it almost to themselves. With its "fine trees and wild nooks and corners" it was a perfect place for the boys to play.

Mrs Oliphant made friends with the neighbours, including the Hawtreys, two brothers and two sisters (Stephen Hawtrey was incumbent of Holy Trinity Church nearby), whom she liked but mocked a little for being "up to their necks in school feasts and soup kitchens and flannel petticoats". Despite having lived with the fear of destitution she was not a woman to give herself to serving soup to the poor. She preferred to organise boating parties and picnics in summer and amateur dramatics in the drawing-room in winter. Howard Sturgis, a schoolfriend of Cyril's and later a minor novelist himself, remembered her as a queenly, gracious figure, recalling that "the little house in Clarence Crescent overflowed with her courtiers". For her these were the "dear and blessed boyish days", which were perhaps the happiest she ever knew. So busy was her social life that writing went on in the evenings and late into the night, after everyone else had gone to bed.

She was becoming well enough known for Queen Victoria to take an interest in her; because of the fuss before her first visit to the Castle Mrs Oliphant wrote to her publisher: "I don't know whether I feel most like the Queen of Sheba or the Pig-faced lady". But the meeting went well: the Queen noted in her *Journal* that "She is very pleasing, so simple, quiet and intelligent". The Queen granted her a pension of £100 a year, and sought her company again from time to time: they had the common bond of widowhood, and because of Victoria's passion for the Highlands Mrs Oliphant's Scottishness appealed too. One evening the family was startled when two soldiers appeared on the doorstep with a parcel. They had brought copies of the Queen's own *Highland Journals*, which came with a modest personal message, that "as a true Scotchwoman the Queen ventures to send them to you". Her librarian later recorded that Mrs Oliphant's were "the only books of which Her Majesty insisted that a complete series should be placed in the Royal Library" (they must have taken up a lot of shelf-space).

After six happy years the character of Mrs Oliphant's life began to change. First came her brother's bankruptcy; at once she generously determined to educate her nephew Frank at Eton too. Then, only a year later a moment arrived which heralded dramatic change. She describes it in her *Autobiography*, using her skills as a novelist to describe an idyllic scene, disrupted by the arrival of a telegram. But this was real life, not fiction:

> We were all assembled, a merry party enough, one summer evening, after an afternoon on the river, at a late meal, when a telegram was put into my hand. I remember the look of the long table and all the bright faces round it, the pretty summer dishes, salad, and pink salmon, and ornamented sweet things, and many flowers, the men and boys in their flannels, the girls in their light summer dresses, everything light and bright.

Oliphant House

For the only time in her life, she says, she did not worry about what was in the telegram. It was from her brother and said "Jeanie [*his wife*] is dead and I am in despair". Now she had to find room for a broken man and two "little white-faced, forlorn children", his daughters. A larger house was needed, and they moved to numbers 8 and 9 Clarence Crescent, now called Oliphant House.

With three more dependent on her pen Mrs Oliphant had to work even harder on what became a nightly "treadmill". Her brother lived on for three years, apparently oblivious to the burden he had placed on his sister. But she was a resilient woman and looked forward to the time when her young men would develop their own careers. "There was no prouder woman in the world than I was with the three", she wrote. In 1874 a photograph was taken of Mrs Oliphant with her sons and nephew on the steps of the house, a location unchanged today. In the light of what was to come it seems ominously prophetic: Mrs Oliphant, wearing widow's weeds and looking older than her forty-six years, gazes anxiously at the camera; Frank sits upright looking into the distance, while Cyril and Cecco loll nonchalantly on or against the stonework. Frank graduated with first class honours from Cooper's Hill engineering college (now part of Brunel University) and entered the Indian Civil Service. Mrs Oliphant was very proud of him and it was a terrible blow when he died of fever in 1879.

But much more sustained grief and distress were to be her lot. Cyril had been a likeable, promising boy who won prizes at school, but when he went to Oxford "my dearest, bright, delightful boy somehow missed his footing". His second class degree was disappointment enough, but worse was to follow. Cyril grew into an idle loafer, caring for nothing but cards and golf, resentful of his nagging mother yet parasitically dependent on her. Through exerting all the influence she could muster she obtained the only employment he ever had, private secretary to the Governor of Ceylon, but it lasted only briefly as the climate made him ill.

Cecco achieved a little more than his brother: he was a natural academic and might have had a career at the British Museum, but he had always been frail and he failed the medical examination. He did write a few articles and, through mother again, was taken on as a part-time assistant at Windsor Castle Library, cataloguing books on heraldry and family history. But this earned him only £10 a month, and so he continued dependent on his mother, and little more appreciative of her support than his brother.

In 1887 Mrs Oliphant wrote:

> Here are all these helpless people, boys who ought to be earning their own living, girls [*her nieces*] who can't but will somehow if I am out of the way, servants, dependants, all accustomed to have everything that is wanted and only me to supply all and I will be 60 in a few months, and my work is failing...

Increasingly as she grew older Mrs Oliphant fell prey to self-pity of this sort.

In 1890 the indolent Cyril suddenly died; terrified for Cecco, whose health was causing growing anxiety, his mother took her remaining child abroad as often as she could, but he grew weaker and thinner and in 1894 he too died. "What a struggle I have had, what endless work and striving, and all ending in those two graves", she wrote sadly. Now the bright Windsor home, "empty, empty, cold and silent", became unbearable. She sold it and moved to Wimbledon, where she longed for death. It came on 25 June 1897, just three days after Queen Victoria's Diamond Jubilee. She was buried in Eton cemetery with her two boys, Queen Victoria herself sending a wreath of white roses, pelargoniums, sweet peas and maidenhair fern, inscribed in her own hand: "As a mark of admiration and regard from Victoria R.I." Her grave is found by looking for the impressive Celtic cross near the entrance: this is, of course, the memorial to Cyril, the son who achieved nothing. His mother's own small stone lies at his feet.

Thus ended a life of "incessant work, incessant anxiety". But was it success or failure? And how far was Mrs Oliphant the author of her own woes? The self-portrait created in the *Autobiography*, a work never prepared for publication, is of a woman burdened both with personal distress and the knowledge that as a writer she had not quite reached the highest rank. In the never-ending struggle to keep her family afloat financially, she had had to sacrifice quality to quantity.

She was particularly sensitive on the subject of George Eliot, the author with whom she was being compared when she first came to Windsor. She wondered if she could have done as well if she too had been kept "in a mental greenhouse and taken care of". George Eliot (Marian Evans was her real name) had a lover, George Henry Lewes, but no children: in March 1862 he "took care of" her by bringing her to the Barley Mow Inn, Englefield Green, as a break from writing her novel *Romola*, and she much enjoyed the walks in the Park. No-one ever nurtured Margaret Oliphant's talent in this way.

Yet even at the beginning of her career, before marriage, she was in the habit of starting a new book immediately the last one was finished. Writing came to her, she said, as "naturally as talking or breathing"—it was an instinctive and necessary activity to her. Whatever her personal circumstances she could probably never have produced the kind of novel that is built up through slow and patient craftsmanship.

Moreover the anxious lifestyle was at least partly a matter of choice. She didn't *have* to send her sons to Eton or hold pretty "pink salmon" parties (Clewer Museum keeps her cook's recipe book, full of fine dishes for entertaining). Mrs Oliphant herself recognised that by making her writing an almost invisible activity she gave her sons the false impression that the good life was achieved without effort.

Much of the *Autobiography* was written in the black misery following Cecco's death: at one point she refers to his coffin being in the next room, so the dreadful mixed emotions of guilt and self-pity come through strongly. Yet her friends always spoke of her as being such good company: "she was one of those people whose presence is even more than a pleasure, it was a stimulus", wrote Annie Ritchie, the novelist Thackeray's daughter. Fortunately it is this Margaret Oliphant, the lively, vigorous-minded Scotswoman, whom we can find in her best books.

Just as she didn't take much part in Windsor life, so Windsor doesn't feature largely in her work, though it is to be found. *The Curate in Charge* is one of her books to have been reprinted; a short novel set in Windsor Forest, it contains pleasing descriptions of the landscape and red-tiled Berkshire cottages. It is the story of two sisters on the threshhold of life who find themselves burdened with the upbringing of twin boys when their improvident curate father dies, and it is an imaginative rewriting of parts of her own life. But Cissie and Mab's story is told with sympathy and humour, and is free from the bitterness which ate at her own heart.

It is said that at Oliphant House it is sometimes possible to glimpse a figure writing, writing, writing, still spinning what she called her "continual webs" of story.

CHAPTER TWELVE

Artist, Architect and Aesthete

Edward Lear (1812-88), Thomas Hardy (1840-1928)
Oscar Wilde (1854-1900), [Mark Twain (1835-1920)]

Edward Lear sketching

EDWARD LEAR came to Windsor in 1853 in a wet and changeable July, to paint a large picture of the view of Windsor Castle from St Leonard's Hill. Lear is best known today as the writer and illustrator of inspired nonsense for children, poems like 'The Owl and the Pussycat', 'The Jumblies' and 'The Dong with a Luminous Nose'. But he made his living as a serious artist. In 1846, the same year that his first *Book of Nonsense* was published, his *Illustrated Excursions in Italy* so impressed Queen Victoria that she asked him to give her drawing lessons, first at Osborne and then Buckingham Palace (when Lear excitedly and naively asked where she had got all the "beautiful things" in a display case, the Queen replied straight-faced, "I inherited them, Mr Lear".)

In fact Lear was largely self-taught, and at the time of his Windsor painting was himself being tutored by the Pre-Raphaelite painter William Holman Hunt. He had agreed to help Lear with his painting techniques in return for Italian lessons.

The Pre-Raphaelite Brotherhood (or P.R.B. as they signed their pictures), was a group of artists including John Everett Millais and Dante Gabriel Rossetti, who banded together in 1849. They were rebels against the rigid tradition of the Royal Academy of teaching art through imitation of old masters such as Raphael; the P.R.B. made truth to nature their guiding principle. Thus Hunt, working at this time on his painting 'The Light of the World' which illustrates Christ's words "Behold, I stand at the door and knock'', set the scene in a moonlit orchard and painted in a real orchard and by real moonlight; when he began the picture in freezing winter weather he built a little shelter and painted through the night with his feet kept warm in a sack of straw.

Hunt could not approve of Lear's practice of developing his oil landscapes in the studio, from water-colour sketches on which he had written colour and identification notes (often in his own idiosyncratic spellings such as ''rox'', ''bloo ski'' and ''korn''). Nevertheless the two men got on well together and though Lear said he'd never make a Brother he would be a son. Hunt, fifteen years his junior, was ''Pa'' or ''Daddy'', and the other Brothers became his uncles. For some weeks the two stayed together at Hastings and Lear learnt to use the clear bright Pre-Raphaelite colours and set his canvas up in the open air in the approved P.R.B. fashion.

But it was one thing to paint where he had the help and encouragement of Hunt, another to go off and work on his own at the Windsor commission. This painting had been ordered by the 14th Earl of Derby, a leading Whig politician who had been Prime Minister for a brief while in 1851 and who at the time occupied the elegant Georgian house so admired by Dorothy Wordsworth. It was the previous Earl who had ''discovered'' Lear when he was young, and the family continued to support the frequently penniless artist for the rest of his life. 'Windsor from St Leonard's Hill' was to be a companion piece to an eight-foot painting of the Acropolis for which Lear had been paid £100.

Lear was easily discouraged; like many comic geniuses he had his dark side, and when he came to Windsor everything seemed to conspire against him. To paint his picture he stayed at the Prince Albert Tavern in Clewer Green (the

The Prince Albert

attractive little pub is still to be found at the junctions of Clewer Green and Winkfield Roads). He wrote from there to Hunt and his letter begins cheerfully enough, chatting about this and that. But when he turns to the painting the tone becomes despairing and he declares that "I sometimes think I cannot go on - & must give up the picture". His problems centred on the attempt to paint in front of his subject and with truth to nature. But like an awkward human subject, nature just wouldn't keep still:

Self Portrait of the artist

> The sky is always beastly blueblack, & I have sent for no end of tubes of the ingredient: & during the week the sun has shone twice. It is therefore utterly impossible to do this view on a strictly P.R.B. principle,—for supposing a tree is black one minute—the next it's yellow, & the 3rd green: so that were I to finish any one part the whole effect would be all spots—a sort of Leopard Landscape.

St Leonard's Hill, which rises higher than the bluff on which the Castle was built, was considered to give the finest view of it, but the artist noticed only that in the inconstant light the main subject of his painting was infuriatingly chameleon-like. His letter continues:

> All the distance also is blue, gray & black—dark & light—by fits,—& the castle which should be in strong light & sharp has been for 2 days jet black—2 more scumbled gray without an iota of detail, & the remaining 2 days wholly invisible. The whole things disgusts me immensely, the more so that as it is to be a portrait I can give way to no remedies of imagination.

His grumbles didn't end with the difficulties of the painting. Playing as he liked to do with the sounds and spellings of words, he admits that he has two "good-sized and crumbfortable rooms" but he also groused that:

> What is more odious to me than all is the absence of nice walks: all dusty roads, & that for miles in all directions.

This reminds us of the difficult road-surfaces before the days of tarmac, but it's clear that Lear was determined to be miserable—he must have noticed that nice walks could be taken in the Great Park nearby. Perhaps he felt that he ought to have been lodged in the great house itself; if so, he would have resented the trudge up a steep dusty road, especially if he had to lug the giant canvas on his back. He was certainly determined not to like Clewer Green, concluding his litany of complaint to Hunt by telling him that "the situation of the place & its noise make it a perfect prison to me".

Despite his troubles Lear carried on with both his picture and his grumbling, though in rather more light-hearted vein, when he left Windsor for Sussex to find some sheep for the fore-ground, which of course P.R.B. doctrine required him to paint from life. To Lord Derby he wrote that:

> Infinite obstacles owing to the size of the picture, the shearing of the sheep, the growth of the lambs &c &c &c &c &c &c, have at last worn me out utterly.

And to Hunt:

> The sheep here are all lame, & entirely driven away. So I shall put in a drove of Apes from the Zoological Society.

If he'd been painting a few years ago he'd have found a troup of baboons nearby at the Safari Park: they'd have given him a lot more trouble than sheep.

The finished picture was displayed in London in 1855, and then the tone of his comments changed from gloom to triumph, even about the trees. He told Lord Derby:

> [I] was much pleased to find that the picture has literally <u>the</u> best place in the whole exhibition... so that all can see it. And the opinions I have from artists whose opinions are valuable to me, are most satisfactory & encouraging, though of course there are many who think that trees should never be painted green, (because they <u>are</u> so), & that all Landscapes should be filled up with trees like Claudes,—(because they <u>ain't</u> so). To such, strict copies of nature are odious.

By then however Lear had decided that absolutely strict copying from nature was not for him, and though he continued to revere Hunt he went back to studio work for large canvases. He always thought that it was these which would establish him in the art world, but it is in fact his water colours which are most highly valued today. Even so it is a pity that the whereabouts of his huge Windsor Castle picture is not now known. And the great house on St Leonard's Hill has gone completely: that familiar to Lear was rebuilt twenty years later in grandiose French chateau style but was itself demolished only half a century later. Only the view remains.

Five years after Lear's unhappy time, the novelist and poet Thomas Hardy first came to Windsor at the age of twenty-two, and likewise with a commission to fulfil. He'd have felt a good deal more enthusiastic about his trip than Lear: when he was a boy one of his favourite books was Harrison Ainsworth's historical romance, *Windsor Castle*, and he once claimed to have fallen in love with a girl simply because she came from Windsor.

The town in the mid-nineteenth century was expanding rapidly, and more churches were needed to match the growth in population. The Prince Consort had laid the foundation stone of the garrison church of Holy Trinity in 1842; another church, to be called All Saints, was planned near his model working men's cottages. Queen Victoria donated £300 towards the building, and the local community contributed £3,400. The architect chosen was the Gothic revivalist Arthur Blomfield; he had in May 1862 taken young Tom Hardy into his sophisticated London office just a week after his arrival in the capital from his native Dorset.

Hardy later described himself as "an isolated student cast upon the billows of London with no protection but his brains", so perhaps he felt more at home in the small town of Windsor. Apart from the interest of the Castle he would also have been conscious as he came into Berkshire that he was entering his grandmother's county. She came from the village of Fawley, and had filled his boyhood with sombre stories of hardship (Hardy was to give the doomed hero of *Jude the Obscure* the surname Fawley).

Blomfield seems to have entrusted Hardy with overseeing much of the work on All Saints: the designs were Blomfield's but it is thought that pencilled notes on them are Hardy's (a few of these designs can be seen today in the church, situated at the junction of Frances and Alexandra Roads).

On 21 November 1863 both men were present at the church's dedicatory service. The foundation stone was laid by Victoria the Princess Royal, who was married to Crown Prince Frederick William of Prussia. The day was a red-letter one for the town: the main streets were hung with flags, bells were rung, and royal salutes fired. A big crowd turned out to watch as the Mayor and Aldermen, preceded by the Mace-bearer, walked in procession to where the area of the church had been covered by an awning (which was as well, since it began to pour with rain during the ceremony). A platform had been raised for important dignitaries, "prettily decorated with flowers, armorial devices

Victoria, Crown Princess of Prussia, laying the first stone of All Saints' Church

and other adornments'' according to the *Windsor Express*. The Bishop of Oxford and the Dean of Windsor were to conduct the service, and ''a goodly number of clergy in full canonicals'' were also present. Just before half-past twelve the cry was raised, ''Here they come!''. The band of the Royal Horse Guards struck up the Prussian National Anthem and the Princess arrived, accompanied by her younger brother and sister, Prince Arthur and Princess Louise.

It was the Princess's twenty-third birthday so she and Hardy were of an age, but the contrast between them was great, he being then quite unknown while she, an intelligent woman of liberal outlook, was seemingly destined to play an important role in shaping European history. Always susceptible to feminine elegance, Hardy must have noted her mauve silk dress, matching bonnet and black velvet mantle trimmed with fur, and been very conscious of the gulf between them. But public occasions made the Princess nervous; when Blomfield handed her the trowel for the ceremony she got her gloves daubed with mortar and in distress thrust it back with a whisper of "Take it, take it!"

Just how big an impression the scene and the Princess made on Hardy was shown a few years later when he was writing his first (unpublished) novel, *The Poor Man and the Lady*, and he included this scene as an episode between the poor architect hero and the squire's daughter with whom he is in love. The manuscript of the novel was afterwards destroyed, but the incident survives in a shorter version of the plot, *An Indiscretion in the Life of an Heiress.*

It seems somehow appropriate that the Princess should have entered Hardy's writing in this small way. The tragic circumstances of her later life, when she and her much-loved husband knew only ninety-nine days as German Emperor and Empress before his death from cancer, and the succession of their militaristic son William II ("Kaiser Bill" of the First World War), might well have been taken by Hardy as an illustration of his belief in malignant destiny.

All Saints' Church in Frances Road

On St Valentine's Day 1885 it was the Irish writer and wit Oscar Wilde's turn to keep an appointment in Windsor. A large audience was expecting him at the Albert Institute in Sheet Street (opened by the Prince of Wales in 1881, it had a lecture theatre for five hundred and other facilities for cultural life). Wilde was to deliver his celebrated lecture entitled 'Dress' ("the hit of the season" according to the *Pall Mall Gazette*). Seats were one shilling (5p) for front seats, half that for those further back. The lecture was scheduled to begin at eight o'clock, but just as audience expectation rose it was announced that Mr Wilde had missed his train and there would be a half-hour delay.

Oscar Wilde

The lecturer's late arrival must have occasioned some tut-tutting, but it's doubtful if anyone went home: Mr Oscar Wilde was a celebrity and everyone would be curious to see and hear him. It would not have been easy for any of them to pinpoint exactly what he was celebrated for: he had certainly published some poems, but the writings for which we remember him today were yet to come. Perhaps it would be best to sum up his achievements thus far as Oscar had done himself when he visited America, and allegedly told a customs official that he had nothing to declare but his genius.

Although Windsor was just another lecture venue on this occasion (and heartily sick of lecturing he was, which may explain a reluctance to get there on time) the town was not unknown to him, as an Oxford friend, Ronald Leveson-Gower, lived at 3 King's Road. Wilde had visited his friend more than once and declared that his house was "one of the most beautiful I ever saw". He aspired to such a home himself, and in 1885 was creating "The House Beautiful" with Constance, his new and equally beautiful wife.

The pursuit of "beauty", or aestheticism, was Wilde's declared principle in life. He was not the only aesthete, for the movement was a rather vaguely-defined extension of Pre-Raphaelitism, but it was Wilde who made it famous. For the man in the street aestheticism was connected with particular objects and colours which the devotees held dear. Blue china was collected and worshipped ("How hard it is to live up to my blue china" was said to be one of Oscar's favourite remarks). Lilies and peacock feathers filled the blue china vases, sun-flowers were a favourite motif, and green and yellow were the admired colours. Oscar worked hard at self-promotion, and was not unhappy when the magazine *Punch* started to caricature him, nor at Gilbert's parody of the "greenery-yallery, Grosvenor Gallery,/Foot in the grave young man" in *Patience*. He may never actually have walked down Piccadilly with a poppy or a lily in his medieval hand, but claimed that "to have made people think one had done it was a triumph".

No wonder then that Windsor wanted to see what Oscar Wilde looked like and listen to what he had to say on dress. Sadly, the *Windsor Express* reporter who attended doesn't tell us what he was wearing. By this time he had given up the knee-breeches and silk stockings which had caused a sensation in America (pictured opposite), but his appearance would have been carefully cultivated to lend weight to his opening statement that "Dress is not merely an art, but one of the fine arts". With his hair styled in Neronic curls he would undoubtedly have seemed dandyish to a provincial audience, yet his costume would not have been recognisably "fashionable" since he argued that fashion was the enemy of beauty of dress.

Wilde had constructed a serious argument on the subject of clothing. He believed that children should be taught to draw the human body to see where its true proportions lie, for fashion gave artificial emphasis to the waist. He analysed the Egyptian, Assyrian and Greek costumes, which unlike modern fashions had lasted for hundreds of years, to see how the best dress fell from the shoulders in a single piece of cloth and was not put together from cut out pieces. Modern dress was, he claimed, a "highly-decorated prison" in which the body moved ill at ease. Moreover it was distorted by tight-lacing: Catherine de Medici, he said, had been accused of many crimes, but none greater than the invention of the corset.

He criticised the expenditure on clothing; his audience laughed when he said that if he were to tell them only the amount that was annually expended on bonnets probably one-half of them would be filled with remorse, the other with despair. Laughter also followed his attack on men's tall silk hats which he claimed had come to be a sign of repectability on weekdays, and absolute orthodoxy on Sundays. In conclusion Wilde made a plea for dress reform: if we endeavoured to make it expressive of art, we should more nearly approach the Greek ideal of the perfectly healthy and beautiful mind.

At the end of the lecture the audience applauded warmly and then went home, the wives no doubt to ease themselves out of their corsets, and the men, with a chaffing word or two about bonnets, to hang up their silk hats ready for the morning. Meanwhile Oscar himself went home to his wife and The House Beautiful.

When he left Oxford Wilde had expressed a determination to be famous, "and if not famous, notorious". He was to achieve both ambitions. In the next ten years he produced most of the writings for which he has won enduring fame: the plays—notably *The Importance of Being Earnest*—his stories for children, and his novel *The Picture of Dorian Gray*, a Faustian tale of a young man who retains his youth and beauty while his portrait gradually reveals the ravages of time and dissipation. But Wilde's own entanglement with a beautiful young man, Lord Alfred Douglas, was to lead to a prison sentence for homosexuality. After two terrible years locked away in conditions of total humiliation Wilde wrote almost nothing more. His only subsequent work was the moving 'Ballad of Reading Gaol' based on his experiences there, and revealing the inhumanity of which men are capable when convinced of their own moral rectitude. Wilde died in exile in Paris, in 1900.

When architecture had been left behind for literature Thomas Hardy was to make other visits to Windsor, and one in particular, in 1907, has been cited in biographies as a good illustration of his unhappy marriage. Thomas and Emma Hardy had been married for thirty years and had succeeded in making each other thoroughly miserable. The vivacious young woman whom Hardy had romantically courted in Cornwall had become cantankerous and domineering. She hated Hardy's later novels *Tess of the d'Urbervilles* and *Jude the Obscure*; she thought them immoral and didn't hesitate to tell him so. But her husband wasn't blameless in the marriage break-up either.

On 22 June that year, just after Hardy's sixty-seventh birthday, a royal garden party on a grand scale was held by King Edward VII on the East Terrace of Windsor Castle and the Hardys were among the nine thousand guests. For Windsor the occasion proved memorable but chaotic: for the first time in its history the town was overwhelmed by motor traffic; crowds lined the route to the Castle to spot celebrities; a small army of photographers darted about, and pickpockets had a field day.

Thomas Hardy

The Hardys travelled in one of the special trains laid on from Paddington in a group which included the French artist Jacques-Émile Blanche. He had just painted Hardy's portrait, and it is from him that the story originates. The King had arranged for carriages to meet trains at the Great Western Railway Station (Windsor Central) and carry guests up to the Castle, but when the Hardy party arrived they found a shortage of carriages. Emma secured a seat in one and offered the remaining place to a woman in their party; she, seeing the frail figure of the writer, demurred and suggested that he should take it instead. But Emma would have none of this: to everyone's embarrassment she made it clear that the walk would do her husband good. The carriage drove off with Emma's green veil streaming like a banner behind and her husband following willy-nilly on foot.

Re-tellings of this incident emphasise how hot the day was and the fatigue the elderly Hardy must have felt. But reports in the *Windsor Express* speak of showers followed by brilliant sunshine and cool breezes, which scarcely suggests insupportable heat. Moreover, Hardy was a countryman well used to walking, and the distance was not considerable.

Perhaps because he trudged inconspicuously up the hill, the *Windsor Express* seems not to have noticed Hardy's presence at the garden party. Everyone who was anyone was there, including almost all the royal family, the Prime Minister (Sir Henry Campbell-Bannerman) and other politicians, naval and military officers, and leading entertainers like Ellen Terry and Dame Nellie Melba. The reporter also spotted another author, the American Samuel Clemens, better known as Mark Twain. He had a ten-minute conversation with the King (the reporter with watch in hand presumably...), during which the King was heard to "laugh heartily" several times (...but not quite close enough to hear the jokes). It was however noted that Clemens was so blind to protocol that he dared to pat the King's arm, and so lucky that he went unreproved.

The day ended as chaotically as it had begun: the bottom of a cab fell out, there were many punctures, and chauffeurs wandered disconsolately around looking for their employers. A great jam developed at the station and the Prime Minister got mixed up with a party of race-goers. How Emma and Thomas Hardy fared on their return journey is not recorded, but if their friends felt that an uphill walk in summer sun could have done the writer no good, at least it did him no harm either: he survived it by twenty years.

Windsor and Clewer from the Curfew Tower, in the middle of the nineteenth century

CHAPTER THIRTEEN

New World Settlers

Henry James (1843-1916), Edith Wharton (1862-1937)
Howard Sturgis (1855-1920)

IN THE NINETEENTH century Atlantic voyages ceased to be the dangerous or desperate undertaking of adventurers or emigrants, as increasing numbers of passenger ships were fitted out to attract the moneyed classes on both sides of the ocean. Dickens visited the New World in order to promote his writing; likewise Americans journeyed to the Old World, often to explore the culture of their ancestors, one which had deeper roots than their own. Some, like the novelist Henry James, came to stay and to give it new growth; those with wealth were often attracted by the idea of becoming country landowners.

Henry James

Two years after Dickens' first voyage to New York, James made his first crossing to Europe when only a baby. His father, also Henry James, from a well-to-do New York family of Irish origin, was one who, like many at a time when scientific discoveries threw doubt on the accuracy of the Old Testament, was seriously disturbed by spiritual uncertainty, and his anxiety was reflected in an unsettled life. In 1843 he made the first of many decisions to ship his wife and two sons to Europe.

After stays in London and Paris, in April 1844 he rented Frogmore Cottage for £4.10.0 a week, plus wages of 8 shillings (40p) for a cook and chambermaid. There he pursued his studies of the *Book of Genesis*. In beautiful spring weather the cottage seemed idyllic; its gardens were enclosed by a six-foot hedge while on the other side the meadows of the Great Park, dotted with oak trees, stretched away into the distance. Sheep, cows and even herds of deer grazed beneath the children's nursery window. (Frogmore Cottage is now found in the private part of the royal grounds, but was then on the public road to Old Windsor. It was not long after the James' family stay that Prince Albert re-routed the roads north and south of the Castle to give the royal family more privacy.)

But a month later the calm was destroyed. Sitting at a table and feeling, he later said, perfectly content, James senior suddenly sensed that some "damned shape" was squatting in the room. He was at once consumed by "insane and abject terror" and struggled vainly to recover self-possession. The experience is probably to be explained as a product of spiritual tension, but the extreme distress which it occasioned remained with him for two years. The family came to refer to the episode as a "Vastation" and it was a shaping influence of the children's early years. Its influence on Henry James junior can perhaps be seen in a story like 'The Turn of the Screw', where ghostly figures threatening the well-being of two young children may be a projection of their governess's state of mind, rather than truly supernatural manifestations.

In fact, despite occurring before the age of awareness, the stay at Frogmore Cottage seems prophetic of what was to come in Henry James' life and fiction. Its setting, an English country house in a parkland landscape, is typical of many of his novels. In *The Portrait of a Lady* of 1881, for example, the story opens with a description of "a peculiarly English picture", tea-drinking on a summer afternoon on the lawn at Gardencourt, a beautiful Tudor red-brick house:

> It stood upon a low hill, above the river—the river being the Thames at some forty miles from London. A long gabled front of red brick, with the complexion of which time and the weather had played all sorts of pictorial tricks, only, however, to improve and refine it, presented to the lawn its patches of ivy, its clustered chimneys, its windows smothered in creepers.

It might almost be Dorney Court near Eton, but the fictional owner of this stately English home is an elderly American. Like so much of James' writing, the novel looks at the interaction of the old world and the new.

James likewise was to make England his adopted country (and at the outbreak of the First World War took British citizenship). It was the era of country house parties, and hostesses frequently invited the distinguished novelist to social gatherings at real Gardencourts. But a house in Windsor to which he often returned belonged, like the fictional one, to a fellow expatriate.

Howard Sturgis was the son of an American banker based in London. He was educated at Eton (where he got to know Cyril Oliphant and his mother) and Cambridge, then, having inherited wealth, stayed in this country and in the 1890s moved into Queensmead Cottage in King's Road. This was an area for prestige development, and the Cottage was built in 1883 near to Queensmead House (now the Brigidine Convent School). "Cottage" was hardly the right word for a house described as a "red-brick neo-Renaissance mansion", and Sturgis changed the name to Queen's Acre, though informally it was known as Qu'Acre, perhaps punning on his New England Quaker background. (The house is still to be found at the junction with Bolton Road, topped by its lion weathervane, but like so many large houses it is now divided into flats, with more flats built in the garden behind.)

James first visited Qu'Acre in 1897, but the best-recorded of his visits are those he paid a decade or so later in the company of a mutual friend and fellow American, the novelist Edith Wharton. The younger woman was known, rather patronisingly since she made much more money out of writing than he, as "the female Henry James". Coming from New York's upper crust she made her reputation with novels of American high society such as *The House of Mirth*. Like James she had travelled widely in Europe in childhood—James called her "the female Ulysses"—and in adult life she crossed the Atlantic every year, husband in tow. (In her last, unfinished novel of the 1930s, *The Buccaneers*, she looked back to this era and took up the Jamesian theme of Americans in Europe, sending four young beauties to England where they rent a pretty cottage at Runnymede, to which male upper-crust youth soon gravitates.)

Edith Wharton

Mrs Wharton got to know the Windsor area well through her visits to Qu'Acre. In her autobiography, *A Backward Glance*, she describes Howard Sturgis as "perfect host, matchless friend, drollest, kindest and strangest of men", and recreates for the reader the experience of entering the house:

> A long low drawing-room; white-panelled walls hung with water-colours of varying merit; curtains and furniture of faded slippery

Architect's drawing of the front of Queen's Acre in 1883

> chintz; French windows opening on a crazy wooden verandah, through which, on one side, one caught a glimpse of a weedy lawn, and a shrubbery edged with an unsuccessful herbaceous border, on the other, of a not too successful rose garden, with a dancing fawn poised above an incongruously 'arty' blue-tiled pool. Within, profound chintz arm-chairs drawn up about a hearth on which a fire always smouldered; a big table piled with popular novels and picture-magazines; and near the table a lounge on which lay outstretched, his legs covered by a thick shawl, his hands occupied with knitting-needles or embroidery silks, a sturdily-built handsome man with brilliantly white wavy hair, a girlishly clear complexion, a black moustache, and tender mocking eyes under the bold arch of his black brows.

As a keen gardener, Wharton is possibly hypercritical about the flowerbeds and weedy lawn.

Sturgis, ambivalently both of large, moustached, masculine appearance yet "a perfect young lady of the Victorian type" as another visitor described him, had put down his pen and picked up knitting needles after some rather thoughtless criticism by James of his novel *Belchamber* (which opens with another seductive portrait of an English country estate). Instead of the complexities of plot and characterisation he turned instead to the patterning of knitting or gold thread embroidery, sitting working away on lawn or by fireside with his dogs beside him, while a constant stream of visitors flowed in and out of the house.

Hospitality was lavish, and many guests appreciated a house "where breakfast in bed was the rule... and there were books in the lavatories". But breakfast in bed could have its disadvantages. Once when trying to get on with her writing in bed and balancing a board with an inkstand on her knees, Edith Wharton knocked the ink over the monogrammed silk sheet. To the housemaid's consternation she insisted on sending it to her host with a note attached:

> Dearest Howard, the book has been going slowly of late; but the stimulating air of Queen's Acre has had its usual effect, and as you will see this morning's chapter has come with a rush.

Sturgis sent back a message of congratulation, and, to the maid's satisfaction, his guest later replaced the sheet.

Sturgis' own daily routine was unvarying. Every morning he set off for "a short toddle" in Windsor Park with his dog Misery and her son: she was so named for having "disgraced" herself by producing an unplanned puppy. For Wharton a walk with Sturgis and the dogs on a cold damp day could be torture, especially when accompanied by Henry James, who would stop every few yards to expound a point, while as soon as he started to move again, Sturgis "was sure to dive into the bushes in pursuit of Misery or her illegitimate offspring".

The glory of a stay at Qu'Acre came later in the drawing-room, when tea was brought in, lamps were lit, and conversation joined. James chose a tea-time image to express his view of Sturgis as "a richly-sugared cake" from which his friends could help themselves while occasionally flinging a slice to outsiders. Ignoring the uncomfortable cannibalistic suggestion of the metaphor it could be said that for Sturgis the cake to be shared was James himself, and he invited many clever young men to talk with and listen to "the Master".

This rather precious assembly would sit with their cups of tea initiating discussion and displaying their wit, while James would stand or pad about, "dominating the room... listening, muttering, groaning disapproval, or chuckling assent to the paradoxes of the other tea-drinkers". Then when the tea tray had disappeared he would stop, lean against the mantlepiece, and launch into elaborate reminiscence, or discussion of great writers past or present. This was what they had come to hear—though since as he got older Henry James became known for the convoluted nature of his sentences, it would have been necessary to concentrate and resist any impulse to doze in the deep armchairs.

With his formidable intellect James had difficulty at times in coming down from its rarefied heights to the level ground of everyday life. Even a staunch admirer like Edith Wharton laughed at some of the consequential absurdities. One anecdote she tells is worth quoting in full. When coming to Qu'Acre she was in the habit of picking James up in her chauffeur-driven car from his home in Rye, and taking him to Windsor. On one occasion when her regular chauffeur was away, they arrived on a dark wet evening and were at a loss to direct him to King's Road. James, spotting an ''ancient doddering man'' gazing at them, leaned out of the car and called out:

> ''My good man, if you'll be good enough to come here, please; a little nearer—so,'' and as the old man came up: ''My friend, to put it to you in two words, this lady and I have just arrived here from *Slough*; that is to say, to be more strictly accurate, we have recently *passed through* Slough on our way here, having actually motored to Windsor from Rye, which was our point or departure; and the darkness having overtaken us, we should be much obliged if you would tell us where we now are in relation, say, to the High Street, which, as you of course know, leads to the Castle, after leaving on the left hand the turn down to the railway station.''
>
> I was not surprised to have this extraordinary appeal met by silence, and a dazed expression on the old wrinkled face at the window; nor to have James go on:
>
> ''In short'' (his invariable prelude to a fresh series of explanatory ramifications), ''in short, my good man, what I want to put to you in a word is this: supposing we have already (as I have reason to think we have) driven past the turn down to the railway station (which in that case, by the way, would probably not have been on our left hand, but on our right), where are we now in relation to...''
>
> ''Oh, please,'' I interrupted, feeling myself utterly unable to sit through another parenthesis, ''do ask him where the King's Road is.''
>
> ''Ah? The King's Road? Just so! Quite right! Can you,as a matter of fact, my good man, tell us where, in relation to our present position, the King's Road exactly is?''
>
> ''Ye're in it,'' said the aged face at the window.

After that it's only fair to let Henry James voice a feeling or two about Edith Wharton. Much though he liked and admired her, the vigour with which she

The 'Chariot of Fire'

swept the aging novelist into her plans left him feeling numbed and breathless. She was always on the go, often in the motor car which he and Sturgis nicknamed the "Chariot of Fire", while she—with a glance at Stravinsky's new ballet—was the awesome "Firebird". James could be open with Sturgis: both were latent if not practising homosexuals, and for them Wharton represented predatory, threatening aspects of female nature. In mock horror James wrote to Sturgis on 20 July 1912:

> My dear, dear Howard, This is a sort of signal of distress thrown out to you... at the approach of the Bird o'freedom—the whirr and wind of whose great pinions is already cold on my foredoomed brow...

Yet, of course, even as he quailed, he did want to be whisked off to Windsor and Qu'Acre.

On this particular visit Mrs Wharton also carried him over to another great estate newly in American ownership, Cliveden, where he stayed for a few days as guest of Mrs Waldorf Astor. There he met poor pregnant Mrs John Jacob Astor whose husband had gone down with the Titanic only four months before, and another forceful female personality, Nancy Astor, later the first woman M.P. to take her seat in parliament. James described her as a "reclaimed barbarian, with all her bounty, spontaneity and charm, too". He had looked forward to seeing Cliveden and strolling in its grounds, and he did enjoy a "beautiful walk on the slopes down to and by [the] river" with Edith, but the "slopes" of Cliveden are steep, and following another such stroll James had a bad attack of angina. They returned to Queen's Acre for a quiet lunch and then Mrs Wharton kindly lent James her car and chauffeur for a "most beautiful and merciful return, by myself, across country, back to Rye".

But a few days later she had joined him there and James was writing plaintively to Sturgis that "The Firebird perches on my shoulder", and protesting that

> All I want is to be let alone, and not to feel myself far aloft in irresistible talons and under the flap of mighty wings and about to be deposited on dizzy and alien peaks.

Sturgis urged him to come to recuperate in peace at Queen's Acre, an invitation gratefully declined. His days of house-partying were over.

In the following year James faced his seventieth birthday, a "grim anniversary", but redeemed by the gift from his friends of a portrait by John Singer Sargent, and a replica seventeenth-century golden bowl in appreciation of his last great novel, *The Golden Bowl.* Edith Wharton had lobbied for the Master to receive the Nobel Prize for Literature in 1911, but as James had not consented to translations of his work it was little known in Europe. However, his achievements were belatedly recognised by his adopted country with the award of the Order of Merit, the insignia of which was brought to him on New Year's Day 1916, two months before his death.

The seventieth birthday portrait is in the National Portrait Gallery, but another Singer portrait, commissioned by Edith Wharton, joined the gallery of those receiving the Order of Merit at Windsor Castle. There it hangs, not far from both Queen's Acre, scene of many congenial visits, and Frogmore, where some of the roots of James' artistic life can be found.

CHAPTER FOURTEEN

Social Rebels

H.G.Wells (1866-1946), Rebecca West (1892-1983), [Lady Florence Dixie 1857-1905]

WINDSOR WAS THE SCENE of both the happiest and the most miserable of the boyhood experiences of H.G.Wells, self-made intellectual, novelist, and advocate of social revolution. The good times were those he had when on holiday at Surly Hall, a riverside inn at Clewer, the bad the month he served at Rodgers and Denyer, a draper's shop in Thames Street. In his fiction he was to draw on memories of both.

Wells was born in Bromley in Kent in Atlas House, a grand-sounding name for a badly-built, inconvenient, smelly and bug-infested shop-cum-home in the High Street. Life for his mother was drudgery and a battle to make ends meet. There was no money for holidays, but she did have a cousin, Thomas Pennicott, a widower at Windsor who had her boys to stay in the summer. For some years he ran the Royal Oak public house opposite Windsor Riverside Station, and did so well that he was able to buy Surly Hall, an inn with lawns running down to the river which was said to be "a great resort for aquatic pleasure parties" (Etonians had christened the inn at a time when it had a notably churlish landlord).

Uncle Tom, as Wells called him, spent lavishly on its rebuilding—too lavishly as it turned out. But for young Bertie, Surly Hall was a paradise where he learnt to punt and row, and was made much of by his cousins Clara and Kate, and the barmaid who pretended to flirt with him. On one occasion the actress Ellen Terry appeared on the lawn, "a delightful vision in fluttering muslin", and Bertie was permitted "to punt the goddess about, show her where white lilies were to be found and get her a great bunch of wet forget-me-nots". At home in Bromley Surly Hall lingered in his memory and on solitary walks he would imagine that it waited for him round every corner.

When he was thirteen Mrs Wells decided that a position in the world had to be found for him and since, as he says in his autobiography, "almost as unquestioning as her belief in Our Father and Our Saviour was her belief in drapers", he had to follow his brothers into the drapery business. Through

The Royal Oak

Uncle Tom Pennicott a trial place was found for him at Rodgers and Denyer (in premises now occupied by the Token House china shop and the Midland Bank). For a £50 apprenticeship premium he would work a seventy-hour week, and in return receive "training", sixpence a week pocket money, and his keep.

In the summer of 1880 Bertie was set down from Uncle Tom's dogcart with his portmanteau, and taken in through a side door. Rodgers and Denyer described themselves as the "leading silk-mercers, linen-drapers, lacemen, court milliners and dressmakers" in Windsor, and were proud of royal patronage, but there was nothing courtly about the dingy accommodation provided for the living-in staff, the poor food, or the long and dreary hours. Wells' first letter home expresses mounting resentment:

> My dear Mother,
>
> Here I am, sitting in my bedroom after the fatigues of the day etc. Cough slightly better & I am tolerably comfortable.
>
> I give you an account of one day's work to give you an idea what I have to do.
>
> <u>Morning</u>
>
> We sleep 4 together every 3 apprentices & 1 of the hands in one room (of course in separate beds).

> We lay in bed until 7.30 when a bell rings & we jump up & put trousers slippers socks & jacket on over nightgown & hurry down & dust the shop etc.
>
> About 8.15 we hurry upstairs & dress & wash for breakfast.
>
> At 8.30 we go into a sort of vault underground (lit by gas) and have breakfast.
>
> After breakfast I am in the shop & desk till dinner at 1 (we have dinner underground as well as breakfasts) & then work till tea (which we have in the same place) & then go on to supper at 8.30 at which time work is done & we may then go out until 10.30 at which hour the apprentices are obliged to be in the house.
>
> I don't like it much for it is not at all like home.

Mother, however, was deaf to the implied plea.

This loathing of underground life was made part of Wells' first successful science-fiction story, *The Time Machine*, published in 1895. In it the Time Traveller reaches a future where the human race has evolved into two forms; one of them, the Morlocks, are descended from the Victorian servant class. After centuries of underground servitude these creatures have become hideously bleached and blind. They still provide food and clothing for the helpless above-grounders, but the Traveller realises to his horror that they care for them as farmers care for cattle: the Morlocks are cannibals. For Wells, writing the story must have been a kind of revenge.

Whenever he could Bertie escaped to Surly Hall, even after work though he found the walk frightening in the dark, especially when it was rumoured that a jaguar kept by Lady Florence Dixie at the Fisheries near Surly Hall had escaped.

[Lady Florence, aunt of Oscar Wilde's love Lord Alfred Douglas, was a travel writer, children's author, and quite a character: in this same year she published a book about her adventures in Patagonia; shortly afterwards she became the first woman war correspondent in the Boer War in South Africa; she was an advocate of women's rights including the right to inherit the throne. She also involved herself in Irish politics, and in 1884 caused a sensation by claiming that while walking by the Thames she had been the victim of an assassination attempt by Irish terrorists disguised as women.]

It simply wasn't possible for a boy as naturally rebellious as Wells to submit to the deadening routine at Rodgers and Denyer. His job was at the cash desk keeping the books, but he disappeared as often as he dared, hiding behind bales of cloth in the warehouse to read or dream. Though he had once come top out of the whole country in a book-keeping exam, the inevitable happened, and at the end of the day the books didn't balance. When older Wells realised that someone must have been watching for his absences and dipping into the cash desk.

At the time he was indifferent to the growing suspicion. It can't have helped that the Summer Sale began on 22 July when, according to Rodgers and Denyer's advertisement in the *Windsor Express*, "the whole stock will be remarked and offered at such prices as will, they trust, effect a ready clearance". When matters came to a head Uncle Tom defended his nephew against charges of pilfering, but there was also a fracas with a junior porter and his employers wanted no more of him. He was "not refined enough" to make a draper.

Something new had to be found. Uncle Tom's brother-in-law, Alfred Williams, who lived in Goswell Lane, had run a school furniture manufactory (he invented the sunken inkwell which many people will still remember in schools), but he had been so improvident that he had lost his position in his own firm. Now he was going as head of a school in Somerset and he offered to take Bertie as a pupil-teacher. So off he went for the experience of being in charge of boys as big or bigger than he, and just as unwilling to learn from him as he from Rodgers and Denyer. But this was a short-lived venture too: after a few months Uncle Alfred's teaching credentials were found to be fraudulent, and both were sent packing.

It was back to Windsor and Surly Hall once more, by rail via Maidenhead, but there he missed his connection and had to stay the night at the Temperance Hotel. Next morning he set out jauntily but was tempted first by a Bath bun and then by a shop where he could get a dozen photographs of himself for one shilling and sixpence (7½p). This left him short of the ticket money to Windsor. So he had to make an arduous trek along the Maidenhead Road with his portmanteau. And when he eventually reached Surly Hall he found that it had changed: "It had become cheerless and almost sinister." Cousin Clara had quarrelled with her father and gone to London. The barmaid had left, Cousin Kate was threatening to go as well, and Uncle Tom was in deep financial trouble, for an inn that was gay and popular with boating people in summer had much less custom out of season. Bertie returned to his mother, no further forward in the world, but wiser in its ways.

Wells later used Surly Hall as a model for the Potwell Inn in his very funny novel *The History of Mr Polly*. Polly, a seedy failed shopkeeper, makes a new life for himself at the Inn with his "fat woman" after a hilarious series of skirmishes with the no-good Uncle Jim. There was to be no such happy ending for Uncle Tom, however. Clara returned unhappy from London and in despair drowned herself. Uncle Tom died. And in 1899 Surly Hall itself disappeared, bought by the Dowager Duchess of Sutherland who lived next door at The Willows, and found it an intrusion on her privacy.

H.G.Wells

Mr Polly was just one of a huge and varied number of books which H.G. Wells produced in later life, including popular science fiction fantasies like *The War of the Worlds,* and novels of social satire like *Mr Polly* and *Kipps*, another story which fictionalises his experiences in the drapery business. Windsor makes several appearances in his novels—and even a startling disappearance in his Utopian fantasy *Men Like Gods*. In it three cars—one containing lightly-disguised versions of the politicians Winston Churchill, Arthur Balfour and Edward Marsh—are driving from Slough to Maidenhead. As they near Taplow, with a view of Windsor Castle in the distance, the cars skid violently. When they come to a stop the occupants find that the Castle has vanished, and they are on a glass road whose verges bear a "gloriously coloured foam of flowers". The possibility of a put-up job is considered ("This road is notorious for nursery seedsmen", says one character, "and sometimes they arrange the most astonishing displays"). Then a leopard strolls out from among the flowers and sits looking at them with a puzzled expression (did Wells remember Lady Florence's jaguar?). They have been transported to another planet, a place which is Wells' vision of a perfect world.

In the early part of this century Wells had a tremendous reputation, not just for his novels but as a thinker, and not just in Britain but throughout the world. He was a social reformer on a grand scale, believing in world government, and the perfectability of life through science (in *Men Like Gods* the Utopians exercise total control over nature). Unfortunately, at a personal level he was known for being disputatious, egoistic, and philandering. He had numerous affairs, most of which were quickly over, but one which lasted for ten years was with the novelist and journalist, Rebecca West. He was to bring her frequently to his favourite hideaway retreat near Windsor, the hotel on Monkey Island.

Rebecca West is one of the foremost women writers of this century. She was made a Dame in 1959 for books like *Black Lamb and Grey Falcon* about the former Yugoslavia (published in 1942), and *The Meaning of Treason* (1947) about Second World War spies. But when she first met H.G. Wells in 1911 she was only nineteen and just beginning in journalism, while he was forty-five and famous, with a wife (the second) and two children.

Her real name was Cicily Fairfield, but thinking that it did not convey the sort of image that she wanted for herself, she adopted the name of one of Ibsen's heroines. She was full of youthful idealism and rebellion, her first published pieces being articles in a radical feminist weekly. Possessed of a sharp wit, she employed it in 1911 in a review of Wells' latest novel *Marriage*, which was critical of conventional marriage. His idea of what should replace it was entirely in terms of male need, and Rebecca contemptuously dismissed the obliging heroine for being "cow-like". Nevertheless Wells was intrigued by her review and invited her to visit him at his home. She found him "one of the most interesting men I have ever met", while he responded to her youth, beauty and intelligence.

Their affair did not begin for some time, but in late 1913 they became lovers. She was his "Panther", he her "Jaguar" (maybe another example of Lady Florence's beast lurking in the roadsides of memory). Wells sent her loving notes, accompanied by "picshuas" of their big-cat selves. "There is NO Panfer but Panfer," he wrote in lovers' childspeak, "and she is the Prophet of the most High Jaguar which is Bliss and Perfect Being". Unfortunately, perfect bliss was shattered when Rebecca became pregnant.

Both despised conventional morality, yet the stigma of unmarried motherhood was such that neither wanted to flout it openly, particularly Wells who, like Dickens, nurtured his public reputation. In the names of Mr and Mrs West, Wells rented a house in out-of-the-way Hunstanton in Norfolk, and there Rebecca waited until her son, named Anthony Panther West, was born on 4 August 1914—an inauspicious birthdate, as it was the day England declared war on Germany. (When the 1914-18 War began it was Wells who described it as "the war that will end war", a phrase that later appeared so inapposite that it helped destroy his reputation as a prophet of the future.)

Monkey Island in the nineteenth century

HG, as Rebecca called him, already had a family and had no intention of divorcing his wife: he wanted Rebecca as an intellectual and physical partner but disliked the nanny\nappy side of life. Rebecca loved the baby and HG, but she also wanted a career and friends; she did not like being cut off in isolated accommodation while Wells, again like Dickens, dashed around between whatever rural retreat she was currently lodged in, his London flat, and his home, where at weekends he regularly engaged in a hectic round of entertaining while she was left literally holding the baby.

In 1916 Rebecca and Anthony stayed for a period at the Riviera Hotel in Maidenhead, and Rebecca asked HG to join them, but he wrote back crossly:

> I wanted you to go to Monkey Island. I could have come there. The Riviera is quite impossible for me... I can't risk being seen in sin at that conspicuous place.

Monkey Island, he said, would have been "cheaper, cleaner, safer and I wanted it". It did not occur to him that Rebecca would have been unhappy, marooned on an island where she couldn't even get to a shop.

Nevertheless, the lovers' happiest times were those together on Monkey Island (so-called for the paintings of monkeys on the wall of what had been the third Duke of Marlborough's fishing-lodge). After the loss of Surly Hall, Wells had adopted the inn on the Thames island near Bray as his sanctuary. Rebecca came to love it too, and in her first novel *The Return of the Soldier*, published in 1918, she makes it the meeting place of a wealthy young man and his first love, the innkeeper's daughter. As the boy reaches the ferry point, a white hawthorn bush where he must ring a bell for the girl to punt across to him, he sees that:

> In front were the dark green glassy waters of an unvisited backwater; and beyond them a bright lawn set with many walnut trees and a few great chestnuts, well lit with their candles, and to the left of that a low white house with a green dome rising in its middle and a verandah whose roof of hammered iron had gone verdigris colour with age and the Thames weather.

With lyrical colour sense she describes leisurely afternoons spent sitting talking on that bright lawn "until the day was dyed with evening blue", and of the twilight "when the green grass seemed like a precious fluid poured out on the earth and dripping over to the river". As the young man leaves he watches the white figure of the girl take the punt

> back over the black waters, mount the grey steps and assume their greyness, become a green shade in the green darkness of the foliage-darkened lawn...

Over such passages West casts the spell of her own happiness on the island.

But as time went on the relationship between Rebecca and HG became increasingly fraught. Wells would have liked to keep Rebecca but on his terms, which did not include marriage. Rebecca on the other hand wanted him to divorce his wife and marry her, for Anthony's sake at least (he had been brought up to call his parents Auntie Panther and Wellsie, a deception which fooled no-one). In 1923, the year of *Men Like Gods* with its "perfect" marriageless scientific world, Rebecca broke off the relationship for good.

Today Monkey Island is still an attractive rendezvous for lovers, though not a cheap one. The M4 spanning the river nearby, and jets roaring overhead, have destroyed the sense of remoteness and peace which Rebecca and HG found there, but if their ghosts haunt anywhere, they are probably to be found as green shades along its tree-lined shores.

CHAPTER FIFTEEN

Lookers Backwards, Lookers Forwards

Osbert Sitwell (1892-1969), Aldous Huxley (1894-1963), George Orwell (1903-50)

IN THE YEARS just before and during the First World War there were three boys enrolled at Eton College who were to become distinguished writers of the twentieth century. Osbert Sitwell was the first of them, arriving in 1907. He writes evocatively about his memories in a chapter of *The Scarlet Tree*, part of his long series of reminiscences. On his first visit, to try on his uniform, he found himself caught by the magical atmosphere of Windsor:

> I remember the day so well, can almost breathe its air, for I had never been in this part of England before, had never seen Windsor, the castle floating like a legendary gothic city upon its hill, or like a fragment from the Arthurian Cycle, yet so solid and robust for all its air of fable.

Osbert Sitwell

About the schooling that followed he was less enthusiastic, telling the reader that he "liked Eton, except in the following respects: for work and games, for boys and masters..."

Most of the enjoyment that Sitwell did find at school came from the river, with desultory boating or bathing in summer, and a particular if brief delight every December when the Thames flooded and games were impossible. Partly for this reason and partly for the wonderful quality of light which the flooding occasioned:

Lupton's Tower, Eton College

> At every break from school, I would run to the meadow's edge to watch with joy the encroaching sheets of water... Alas, these transient and shimmering meres, which brought to all things such an enhancement of their quality, seldom existed for more than four or five days. With a sorrow equal to my previous joy, with a sense, too, of life going flat again, I saw these calm and gentle waters begin to recede, until they had gone, leaving behind them only a thin layer of mud, and a lingering faint scent, enduring a day or two, of moss and weed...

While the taming of the Thames is a relief for householders, this annual flooding and the shining stretches of water in the meadows, so long known to those who lived along its banks, is a part of the cycle of the seasons which we have lost.

Sitwell records that he often saw the king, Edward VII, as he drove to Windsor, and he heard him speak when he came to open the school library built as a memorial to Etonians who had died in the Boer War, and opened in the presence of many who were to die in the war to come. He says that the King's voice possessed "a very individual and husky warmth", and that there was "a geniality in its sound, as of one who found in life the utmost enjoyment". On another occasion the King brought his nephew, the German Kaiser, to Eton; Sitwell sardonically notes that

> the Kaiser obtained for us a week's extra holiday—the only debt, I think, that Etonians of my generation ever owed him. Even on this, the

> interest amounted to usury, for seven years later he took away from us by the sum of his actions at least four years of our lives, and in many instances the whole period that remained.

With hindsight, so much that happened during this state visit to Windsor Castle seems ironically overladen. It took place in November 1907 and it was a very grand occasion indeed, with the town on its mettle for a man who liked parades. The station was "profusely" decorated with flags, welcome signs, flowers and foliage, and as the Emperor stepped out of his train his Guard of Honour was formed of "plumed officers in gorgeous uniforms... chosen from the finest specimens of manhood in the ranks of the Horse Guards". The Mayor of Windsor presented him with an elaborately illuminated address, which Queen Victoria's eldest grandson accepted with the words: "We thank you very much, Mr Mayor. It always feels like coming home again to come to Windsor." Enthusiastic crowds lining the streets included a detachment of the Eton College Volunteers.

The week which followed alternated grand banquets and entertainments with what royalty really liked to do: go shooting. On the first shoot, at the Flemish Farm, the Emperor bagged seven hundred birds; by tact or chance the King killed slightly fewer. Sunday luncheon at the Castle was attended by a record number of European royals: most of them—including the Kaiser himself—would lose their crowns as a result of the conflagration to come.

By coincidence only a week earlier it had been announced that the measurements of all Eton boys were to be taken, to answer the question "Does our system of outdoor games produce on average a finer and more powerful individual than the more martial exercises of German boys?" If the theory had any reality, Osbert Sitwell's measurements must have been puny, given his absolute dislike of sports. He managed to persuade his father to let him leave Eton in the summer of 1909, returning only to collect the standard leaving present of a volume of Gray's poems. These included his 'Ode on a Distant Prospect of Eton College' and their far from encouraging lines for a school-leaver:

> Alas, regardless of their doom,
> The little victims play !
> No sense have they of ills to come,
> Nor care beyond today...

For that war-doomed generation, Gray was sadly prophetic.

Aldous Huxley

A year later, in 1910, Edward VII died, and his body was brought from London to be interred in St George's Chapel. Once again boys from the Eton College Officers' Training Corps played a part, and amongst them was the teen-aged Aldous Huxley. Facetiously he wrote to his cousin that he had been "holding an official position in lining the route and keeping the rabble back with the butt end of my rifle". Huxley seems to have been quite happy at school, judging from his cheerful letters full of schoolboy jokes, though fellow students found the lanky young man awesomely intelligent, clearly destined to be "a superior being".

In 1911, however, when he was sixteen, Huxley had to leave school after an eye-infection left him almost completely blind. With courage and determination he mastered Braille and continued his studies, telling his cousin that "there's one great advantage in Braille, you can read in bed without getting your hands cold".

There was another advantage: when war came in 1914 there was no question of Huxley joining his companions from the Officers' Training Corps on the western front. By then he was studying at Oxford: he had recovered partial sight, but still needed a magnifying glass for all his reading. In 1916, while many of his age were preparing for the Battle of the Somme, Huxley took his final exams and graduated with a first class degree.

Finding employment was difficult, but with so many men in the forces, even the best of schools had difficulty at this time in recruiting staff, so Eton College was ready to employ someone already making his mark in the literary world (some of the poetry he was writing was appearing in a magazine run by the Sitwell family), even if he was half blind. So in 1917 Huxley became a master at his old school, lodging at the Old Christopher in Eton High Street. But since he had no enthusiasm for teaching, and was unable to see what was happening at the back of the class, his lessons were generally disastrous. One of his pupils later wrote:

> Poor Aldous ! He must have been one of the most incompetent schoolmasters who ever faced a class...[it was] impossible to hear more than an occasional word of what was read or said for the general tumult was indescribable.

With nobody on the staff with whom whom he had anything in common, he could only endure Eton's "grim solitudes".

Yet there were a few who responded to Huxley's teaching, among them a boy called Eric Blair, who was fascinated by his use of words. A contemporary recalled that Blair would

> make us note Aldous's phraseology, "That is a word we must remember," we used to say to each other... The taste for words and their accurate and significant use remained.

Eric Blair was the future George Orwell, a writer noted for the precision and clarity of his language.

It isn't easy to recognise the future thin-faced classless socialist Orwell, author of *Animal Farm* and *Nineteen Eighty-Four*, in plump-featured Eric of old Eton photographs. But in one shot taken at the bathing station Athens, he defies authority with a cigarette fixed to his lower lip, and there the later anti-authoritarian adult can be seen. Eric's record at Eton was not distinguished: he did not go on to Oxbridge, and when he began his writing career he adopted a new name and a determination to "live down" his Eton past.

Orwell rarely mentions Eton in his writings, but in an article in the left-wing journal *Tribune* he can be seen drawing on his schoolboy memories

> One day I was walking past Windsor Castle when a sort of electric shock seemed to go through the street. People were taking their hats off, soldiers springing to attention. And then, clattering over the cobbles, there came a huge, plum-coloured open carriage drawn by four horses with postilions. I believe it was the first and last time in my life that I have seen a postilion. On the rear seat, with his back to the carriage, another groom sat stiffly upright, with his arms folded... I hardly noticed the Queen, my eyes were fixed on that strange, archaic figure at the back, immobile as a waxwork, with his white breeches that looked as though he had been poured into them, and the cockade on his top hat. Even at that date (1920 or thereabouts) it gave me a

wonderful feeling of looking backwards through a window into the nineteenth century.

George Orwell

Orwell's biographer Bernard Crick comments, "And so might the postilion have thought if he had looked at the Eton boy". However, it can further be said that in his desire to make a political point about the monarchy Orwell is guilty of historical distortion which, if minor, is still the sin he found most obnoxious in totalitarian governments.

In the way he presents the incident as an unexpected event, Orwell manages to suggest that Queen Mary rode out in a plum-coloured carriage with postilions quite as an everyday matter. But of course she didn't. Almost certainly the event around which Orwell builds his anecdote did not occur in "1920 or thereabouts" as he disingenuously suggests, but was her drive through Windsor on 28 April 1917 during the war, which she made as part of the St George's Day celebrations and at the particular request of the Mayor of Windsor, to help raise funds for local charities. The Queen, with Princess Mary, Prince George (later George VI) and Prince Henry, drove out in the coach drawn by four greys and with two postilions. Church bells rang out, the streets were decorated with the flags of the allies, school-children (no doubt Eric Blair among them) lined the route, and more than £300 was raised for the various charities.

For Windsorians a bit of pageantry at this time was a welcome distraction from the horrors of war. These weren't easy to ignore: the spring offensive had begun, and just next to the account of the procession in the *Windsor Express*, is a column devoted to local war deaths and injuries. One such casualty from the very heart of Windsor was twenty-five year old Second Lieutenant W.W. Green of Peascod Street, killed "instantaneously" on the German barbed wire on Easter Monday, while rallying his men. (Maybe the death was indeed instantaneous, but soldiers knew that this word was often army cover-up for a long, lonely and agonising death out in no-man's-land.)

If one can fault Queen Mary in her morale-boosting ride round the town it is in her visit to see wounded soldiers at King Edward VII Hospital. There the plum-coloured coach merely circled the sick soldiers, who were laid out in their cots on the grass. Fortunately the weather kept fine, "apart from a light shower". There could be no clearer illustration of the difference between royalty then and today.

When the war at last ended in November 1918, Osbert Sitwell, who had faced his share of horrors but survived, wrote:

> No-one, then, who had not been a soldier, alive on the morning of the 11th of November 1918, can imagine the joy, the unexpected, startling joy of it...

Aldous Huxley, however, had some months to go before release from his misery at Eton.

In the years that followed, when euphoria turned to disillusion as it became clear that the "war to end all war" had settled nothing, Huxley and Orwell, master and pupil, were each to produce powerful and disturbing novels of prophecy. Huxley's *Brave New World* was published in 1932, and Orwell's *Nineteen Eighty-Four* in 1949, following another world war.

Huxley says that *Brave New World* was partly a corrective to Wells' complacent view of perfectability through science in *Men Like Gods*. He creates such a "perfect" world, setting it six hundred years hence, when all the old causes of human misery have been removed. To avoid the traumas of marriage and family life, humans are mass-produced in bottles on a conveyor belt, children are educated through indoctrination, promiscuous sex is a duty, and all anxiety banished by a happiness-inducing drug. Life is one long and soulless round of fun and games.

At one point Huxley takes his characters in a helicopter to a transformed Eton, where Lupton's Tower has become a fifty-two storied building, and instead of Henry VI a "chrome-steel statue of Our Ford" stands in the quadrangle (Henry Ford, creator of the factory-produced Model T Ford is founder and god of this society). Huxley obviously enjoyed the joke, but his further revelation that *girls* are enrolled at the College is no longer far-fetched. Nor are his helicopters, skyscrapers, drugs, or manipulated human births. When he describes how all eyes were drawn to "the majestic buildings of the

Slough Crematorium'' whose four tall chimneys are a floodlit landmark, we may laugh at the exaggeration, but can't feel the weirdness as Huxley's first readers could. In many ways it is only in degree that we are separated from his brave new world.

By contrast, the chilling threat of Orwell's totalitarian *Nineteen Eighty-Four*, published as the Cold War intensified, seems to have receded. It was not long after we had passed the real 1984 that the Berlin Wall came down and dictatorial communism collapsed. Gone, at least for now, are the threat of Big Brother and the Thought Police.

But, however ''archaic'', monarchy and Castle are still in place at the end of the century—hanging on, maybe, but then the pattern through history has been one of see-saw. What would Pepys or Evelyn have given for Charles II's chances in 1649? Who could be confident that George III would keep his throne when the French Revolution swept Louis XVI from power? If Orwell had looked and thought with a little less bias he might have used the same words and without ironic intent written that the Queen in her coach and four gave a ''wonderful feeling of looking backwards through a window into the nineteenth century''... and the eighteenth, seventeenth, and so on right back to the origins of town and castle on a chalk cliff beside a mighty river nine centuries ago. For most writers who have helped to shape our perception of history, and readers who have responded to their words, the past is a valued legacy to be treasured and handed on to the readers and writers of the next millenium.

Geoffrey Chaucer

Select Bibliography

Writers:

AMOR, Anne Clark, *William Holman Hunt: The True Pre-Raphaelite*, London 1989.

AYLMER, Felix, *Dickens Incognito*, London 1959.

BARRETT, Charlotte, *The Diary and Letters of Madame D'Arblay* (with Preface and Notes by Austin Dobson), Volumes 2-4, London 1904-5.

BEDFORD, Sybille, *Aldous Huxley: A Biography*, Volume 1, 1894-1939, London 1973.

BINGHAM, Caroline, *The Stewart Kingdom of Scotland*, London 1974.

BOSWELL, James, *The Life of Samuel Johnson*, London 1925.

BREWER, Derek, *Chaucer and His World*, London 1978.

CHAMBERLIN, E.R., (ed.), *William Cobbett: Rural Rides*, London 1982.

CHERRY, Alastair, *Princes, Poets and Patrons: The Stuarts and Scotland*, Edinburgh 1987.

COGHILL, Mrs Harry (ed.), *Autobiography and Letters of Mrs Margaret Oliphant* (with an introduction by Q.D. Leavis), Leicester 1974.

CRICK, Bernard, *George Orwell: A Life*, London 1980.

DAVENPORT, Hester, 'Edward Lear at Clewer Green', in *Windlesora 13*, 1994.

DE BEER, E.S. (ed.), *The Diary of John Evelyn*, London 1959.

DE SELINCOURT, Ernest (ed.), *The Early Letters of William and Dorothy Wordsworth*, Oxford 1935.

DOLLERY, Ellen, 'Thomas Hardy and All Saints' Church', in *Windlesora 6*, 1987.

DOODY, Margaret Anne, *Frances Burney: The Life in the Works*, New Brunswick 1988.

DUNN, Jane, *Moon in Eclipse: A Life of Mary Shelley*, London 1978.

DYSON, Hope and TENNYSON, Charles, *Dear and Honoured Lady: The Correspondence of Queen Victoria and Alfred Tennyson*, London 1969.

EDEL, Leon, *Henry James: The Master 1901-1916*, London 1972.

EDEL, Leon (ed.), *Henry James: Letters,* Volume IV, Cambridge (Massachusetts) and London, 1984.

EDWARDS, Philip, *Sir Walter Ralegh*, London 1953.

EHRENPREIS, Irwin, *Swift: The Man, His Works, and the Age*, Volume 2, *Dr Swift*, London, 1967.
ELLMANN, Richard, *Oscar Wilde*, London 1987.
FARR, Evelyn, *The World of Fanny Burney*, London 1993.
GITTINGS, Robert, *Young Thomas Hardy*, London 1975.
GITTINGS, Robert, *The Older Hardy*, London 1978.
GITTINGS, Robert and MANTON, Jo, *Dorothy Wordsworth*, Oxford 1985.
GLENDINNING, Victoria, *Rebecca West: A Life*, London 1987.
HEDGES, David, 'Charles Knight of Windsor', in *Windlesora 6*, 1987.
HEMLOW, Joyce, *The History of Fanny Burney*, Oxford 1958.
HOLMES, Richard, *Shelley: The Pursuit*, London 1974.
HOUSE, Madeline and STOREY, Graham (eds.), *The Collected Letters of Charles Dickens*, Volumes 2 and 6, Oxford 1969 and 1988.
HARDY, Florence Emily, *Life of Thomas Hardy*, London 1928.
JAY, Elizabeth (ed.), *The Autobiography of Margaret Oliphant: The Complete Text*, Oxford 1990.
JONES, Frederick L. (ed.), *The Letters of Percy Bysshe Shelley*, Oxford 1964.
KAPLAN, Fred, *Dickens: A Biography*, London 1988.
KAPLAN, Fred, *Henry James: The Imagination of Genius*, London 1992.
KEENE, Dennis (ed.) *Henry Howard Earl of Surrey, Selected Poems*, London, 1985.
KETTON-CREMER, R.W., *Horace Walpole: A Biography*, London 1940.
KNIGHT, Charles, *Passages of a Working Life*, London 1864.
LATHAM, R.C. and MATTHEWS, W. (eds), *The Diary of Samuel Pepys*, Volumes 5, 6 and 7, London 1972.
LEWIS, R.W.B., *Edith Wharton: A Biography*, New York 1975.
LEWIS, R.W.B., *The Jameses: A Family Narrative*, London 1991.
LEWIS, W.S. *Horace Walpole's Correspondence*, Oxford and New Haven, 1937-83.
MACK, Maynard, *Alexander Pope: A Life*, New Haven and London, 1985.
MACKENZIE, Norman and Jeanne, *The Time Traveller: The Life of H.G. Wells*, London 1973.
MARTIN, Robert Bernard, *Tennyson: The Unquiet Heart*, Oxford 1983.
MILLGATE, Michael, *Thomas Hardy: A Biography*, Oxford 1982.
MORRIS, Christopher (ed.), *The Illustrated Journeys of Celia Fiennes*, London 1982.

NOAKES, Vivien, *Edward Lear: The Life of a Wanderer* (revised edition), London 1979.
NOAKES, Vivien, *Edward Lear 1812-1888*, London 1985.
NOAKES, Vivien (ed.), *Edward Lear: Selected Letters*, Oxford 1988.
OLIVER, H.J. (ed.), *The Merry Wives of Windsor* (Arden Shakespeare), London 1971.
PEACOCK, Thomas Love, *Memoirs of Shelley*, London 1909.
PEARSALL, Derek, *The Life of Geoffrey Chaucer*, Oxford 1992.
RAY, Gordon N., *H.G.Wells and Rebecca West*, London 1974.
ROBINSON, Denys Kay, *The First Mrs Thomas Hardy*, London 1979.
ROWSE, A.L., *Ralegh and the Throckmortons*, London 1962.
ROYAL ACADEMY OF ARTS, *Edward Lear*, London 1985.
SITWELL, Osbert, *The Scarlet Tree*, London 1946.
SMITH, Grover, *Letters of Aldous Huxley*, London 1969.
TOMALIN, Claire, *The Invisible Woman: The Story of Nelly Ternan and Charles Dickens*, London 1990.
WEBER, Carl, *Hardy of Wessex*, London 1965.
WHARTON, Edith, *A Backward Glance: An Autobiography*, London 1934.
WILLIAMS, Harold (ed.), *Jonathan Swift, Journal to Stella,* Volumes 1 and 2, Oxford 1974.
WILLIAMS, Merryn, *Margaret Oliphant*, London 1986.

History local and national:

BOND, Maurice, *The Story of Windsor*, Newbury 1984.
FARRAR, Henry, *Windsor Town and Castle*, Chichester, 1990.
GIROUARD, Mark, *Windsor: The Most Romantic Castle*, London 1993.
GREGG, Edward, *Queen Anne*, London 1980.
HIBBERT, Christopher, *The Court at Windsor: A Domestic History*, London 1964.
HARWOOD, T.E., *Windsor Old and New*, London 1929.
HUNTER, Judith, *The Changing Face of Windsor: The Beginnings*, Slough 1977.
HEDLEY, Olwen, *Windsor Castle* (revised edition), London 1994.
HUGHES, G.M., *Windsor Forest*, London 1890.
LONGFORD, Elizabeth, *Victoria R.I.*, London, 1964.

MACNAGHTEN, Angus, *Windsor and Eton in Georgian Times*, 1975.
MACNAGHTEN, Angus, *Windsor and Eton in Victorian Times*, 1976.
MORSHEAD, Sir Owen, *Windsor Castle*, London 1957.
ROONEY, Sheila and Pat, *St Leonard's Hill Windsor*, Windsor 1991.
ROWSE, A.L., *Windsor Castle in the History of the Nation*, London, 1974.
SOUTH, Raymond, *The Book of Windsor: The Story of a Royal Town*, Chesham, 1977.
TIGHE, Robert Richard, and DAVIS, James Edward, *Annals of Windsor* (Volumes 1and 2), London 1858.
WINDSOR, SLOUGH & ETON EXPRESS, editions for 15.ii.1840, 28.xi.1863, 17.vii.1880, 21.ii.1885, 11.v.1889, 9.ii.1901, 29.vi.1905, 2, 9, 16 and 26.xi.1907, 28.iv.1917.
WINDSOR CHRONICLE, edition for 2.7.1897.
WINDSOR LOCAL HISTORY Publications Group, *The Streets of Windsor and Eton*, Windsor 1988.

Charles Knight

Writers' Windsor

A Literary Walk

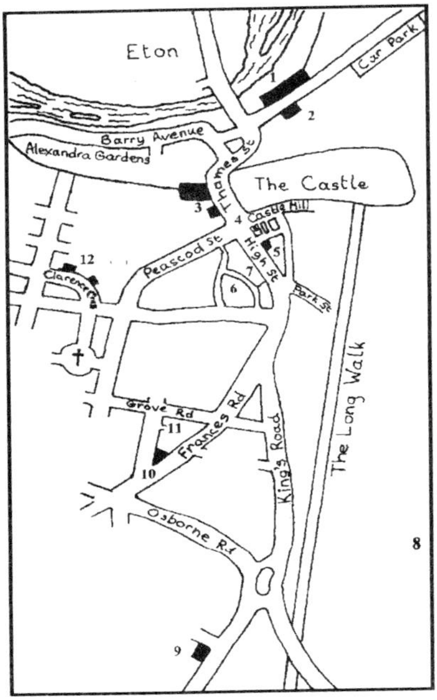

(The walk, of about three miles, is best undertaken on a Tuesday, Wednesday or Thursday morning, when All Saints' Church should be open between 10 and 12 o'clock (you can check first by phoning the church warden, Angela Drewett, 01753 861980).

Start the walk at Windsor and Riverside Station (1). The South Western Station (as it was then called) with its fine brickwork opened in 1851, and was one of the stations useful to Charles Dickens in the 1860s when he set up the actress Nelly Ternan in a cottage in Slough. He would walk over the fields and catch his morning train for London from here or Datchet Station. Opposite the station, comfortably tucked beneath the Round Tower, is the Royal Oak pub (2) where H.G. Wells spent happy boyhood holidays with his Uncle Tom Pennicott.

Thames Street has to be tackled next, following in the path of almost all the writers in this book, though not all walked up it—Chaucer will have ridden his little horse, Swift arrived in style in a coach with the chief ministers of the land, and Henry James and Edith Wharton swept up in the Chariot of Fire. The trudge recalls Hardy's lines about a walk he and Emma once took up another steep hill at Boscastle, climbed 'foot-swift, foot-sore\By thousands more'. On that occasion they had got down from their pony-drawn cart to lighten its load, but at Windsor, when they arrived at the Great Western Station by train for the great garden party given by Edward VII, she told him to walk while she secured a place in a coach.

Just by the station entrance is the Hart and Garter (3), on the site where Shakespeare found the Garter Inn, and Pepys stopped for lunch on the day of his memorable visit in 1666. High up on the building can be seen the name The White Hart by which Dickens knew it when he stayed there in 1841 to recuperate from an illness, long before the days of an actress mistress.

As you walk on with the Castle walls on your left—for Charles Knight, and writers before him, they were obscured by a row of houses in the ditch—you can see Knight's birthplace straight ahead (4). There is a plaque on the wall. At the time of his childhood the stench at this point, with open drains disgorging from the Castle, must have been overwhelming, and you would not have wanted to linger in the narrow streets behind the Guildhall (5), but you might like to explore them or seek refreshment. In St Alban's Street at the back was once the house where Fanny Burney stayed with Mrs Delany.

On the opposite side of the High Street the Midland Bank and the Token House now occupy the site where Messrs Rodgers and Denyer had their highly-respectable draper's business, too respectable and far too oppressive for their boy apprentice Bertie Wells, who hated their rigid rules and mean-spirited provision for staff.

Cross the road and go down Peascod Street to the narrow Acre Passage leading to Bachelors' Acre (6). This historic site, soon to get a face-lift, would have been very unattractive when sewage drained into it in Charles Knight's time. He is buried at the back of the old burial ground (7) though the lettering on his grave is unreadable. A plaque is to be placed nearby on the wall, and you can see the Charles Knight Memorial Gates at the end of Madeira Walk, placed there in his memory by his son.

Follow the passage signed to the High Street, which brings you out opposite the parish church (was it here that the great Dr Johnson declined to attend service and instead lay down on a tombstone?) Turn right, and at the junction cross to Park Street, from where if you look up at the buildings on your left you can see the statue of Prince Albert, all that remains of the Royal Albert Institute where Oscar Wilde gave his well-attended lecture in 1885.

Elegant Park Street was once the main highway to Staines, and so the route taken by Horace Walpole when he visited The Priory at Old Windsor, but now it leads just to the peace and noble views of the Long Walk (8). We can only be thankful that Prince Albert created a new road and enabled us to enjoy the walk in tranquillity. Swift thought it "delicious" and walked here frequently, once with Esther Vanhomrigh, "Vanessa". Celia Fiennes admired it from the ramparts of the Round Tower, Fanny Burney and Dorothy Wordsworth walked here and, if he can be believed, Dickens flung himself down in the February mud to register his distress at Queen Victoria's marriage.

Follow in their footsteps down the Walk, looking back now and then at the Castle behind you. On the left you can glimpse Frogmore Mausoleum where Queen Victoria once gave her Poet-Laureate Tennyson a conducted tour of her greatest monument to Albert. Somewhere in the trees is the Frogmore cottage in which Henry James stayed in babyhood. Continue to the junction with Albert Road, where the noise of traffic again dominates.

Ahead is the Copper Horse, and on the right King's Road, where on a dark, wet night James got wordily lost with Edith Wharton. Cross to the Ascot Road: a short detour brings you to Queen s Acre (9), home then of Howard Sturgis, which the novelists were trying to reach. In the nearby parkland the elderly bachelors would potter about while Edith Wharton fretted at their slowness. She once appalled the sedentary Sturgis by suggesting that he might like to come out with her one summer afternoon for a walk to Eton: "Walk down to Eton with you? *Now*—at this hour of the day? But you went for a walk this morning; and you've been motoring all over the place all the afternoon... and now you're actually suggesting that I should walk all the way to Eton with you before dinner?" No doubt Sturgis and James would baulk at this walk too.

Retrace your steps and walk down Osborne Road—with a fine Castle view to your right—to the pedestrian crossing. Turn the corner to Frances Road and find All Saints' Church (10) in front of you. As a young architect, Thomas Hardy was given responsibility for overseeing the building of the church. Though severe in appearance outside, the inside is pleasingly proportioned and decorated, and you can see architectural drawings and notes in Hardy's own hand mounted on the walls. These were found only in the 1970s. They were in dirty rolls behind the organ of the parish church, and were recognised by Hardy-enthusiast Ellen Dollery, and later authenticated by an expert.You should be able to refresh yourself here with tea, coffee or hot chocolate.

Set off again past Prince Consort Cottages (11), built by Prince Albert to be model working men's cottages.Turn left into Grove Road, right into St Leonard's Road, left to the garrison church, then along Trinity Place. Cross the main road to Clarence Crescent where Margaret Oliphant lived, first at number 6, then at 8-9, which is now called Oliphant House (it is to be given a commemorative plaque in 1997, the centenary of her death). The "Plantation", the community garden where her boys played, can be seen, but is tantalisingly out of bounds for all but residents.

Turn right out of the Crescent and keep going straight, under the railway arches, until you reach Alexandra Gardens and the river bank. Until the building of the railways much of this area of Windsor was covered with slum housing. Now a leisurely stroll with fine views (ignored by the three men in Jerome K. Jerome's boat) brings you to Eton Bridge and back to the Royal Oak, and perhaps a well-earned drink.

PUBLICATIONS BY

WINDSOR LOCAL HISTORY PUBLICATIONS GROUP

Windlesora - Annually

No. 14 includes : The Thames Towpath Controversy by **Raymond South** - Lord Gowrie VC - "Curtain Up" at the Theatre Royal - Windsor Model Aero Club - the mystery of "The Man on the Memorial" - £2

No. 15 (November 1996) celebrates the twenty-first anniversary of the foundation of the group. Articles will include : **Alice in Wonderland**: the Windsor Connection - The Marquis d'Harcourt by **Sheila Rooney** - Perdita Robinson by **Hester Davenport** - Topham Foote and Thomas Reeve by **Leslie Grout** and a review of this book by **Raymond South**.

JUDITH HUNTER and Others

The Streets of Windsor and Eton

(2nd Edition edited by Pamela Marson - 2nd Reprint) £2

Windsor in the Last Century

Six Views of the Town by A.T. BARBER

Originally published 1897 (a Windlesora Reprint) 1990 £1

SHEILA ROONEY

Fires of Windsor Castle

(2nd Reprint) 1993 £5.95

Further details of all these books available from:

256 Dedworth Road . Windsor . SL4 4JR. Tel: (01753) 866835